NICK FALDO

IN PERSPECTIVE

NICK FALDO

IN PERSPECTIVE

JOHN HOPKINS

London
GEORGE ALLEN & UNWIN
Boston   Sydney

**George Allen & Unwin (Publishers) Ltd,
40 Museum Street, London WC1A 1LU, UK**

George Allen & Unwin (Publishers) Ltd,
Park Lane, Hemel Hempstead, Herts HP2 4TE, UK

Allen & Unwin Inc.,
9 Winchester Terrace, Winchester, Mass 01890, USA

George Allen & Unwin Australia Pty Ltd,
8 Napier Street, North Sydney, NSW 2060, Australia

First published 1985

ISBN 0 04 796109 0

Set in 12 on 14 point Eras Book by Bedford Typesetters Limited, Bedford
and printed in Great Britain by Mackays of Chatham

For
Susi, Rhys and Annelies

Contents

List of Illustrations

Faldo shares a joke with Jimmy Tarbuck
And just occasionally there's a prize worth winning too!
Faldo with Peter Oosterhuis in the 1981 Ryder Cup
at Walton Heath
Faldo and Sandy Lyle
Author, John Hopkins posing at The Open, St Andrews, 1984
John Simpson at the 1983 Masters
Nick Faldo and Gill Bennett
Nick Faldo with his caddie David McNeilly
Sometimes it's a pleasant walk in the countryside
Sometimes it's not: (a) Signing autographs
(b) Landscape putting
(c) Using a reversed club
(d) Spot the ball
(e) A record round at the Colgate PGA Championship, 1979
(f) At the short 14th on the West Course at Wentworth
(g) Winning the Car Care Plan for the second year
in succession

Acknowledgements

Robert Green of **Golf World**, David Robson of the **Sunday Times** and Derek Wyatt of George Allen & Unwin were very helpful to me while I was writing this book. My thanks to them.

JOHN HOPKINS
London
February 1985

Introduction

I have watched Nick Faldo play golf on courses as far apart as Stockholm, St Andrews and San Diego but it was only when I was gathering material for this book that I visited him at home and saw him in an environment of his own creating. I arrived at his newly-acquired house one November afternoon as dusk was gathering and snow threatened to fall from plump grey clouds overhead.

I pressed the bell and an enormous figure loomed the other side of the frosted glass front door. It swung open to reveal Faldo dressed casually in chocolate brown sweater and shirt, brown corduroys, slippers and, on his left wrist, a chunky gold Rolex. 'Ah, there you are,' he said. 'Come in and look around. We're nearly finished.'

Running down the thickly-carpeted stairs, Faldo led the way to a room dominated by a snooker table that doubled up as a dining table. He picked up a cue and absent-mindedly shattered a cluster of balls. On one wall hung the shield from the Heritage, his first victory in the US. Spread across almost the whole of another wall was a huge, glass-fronted cabinet containing cups, tankards and spoons. Beside the door into the kitchen was a smaller cabinet housing two of Faldo's most prized possessions: a cup no taller than a fountain pen that he had won as a junior at John O'Gaunt Golf Club. It was his first victory, his rounds were 71 and 77 and his handicap was seven; his other favoured possession was a honey-coloured wooden box containing a set of 19th century slides of animals and plants that he had bought for twelve pounds in an antique shop.

He stretched out an arm and took down something from the back of a higher shelf. To my surprise I noticed it wasn't a golf trophy but an otter crafted in glass and no bigger than his middle finger. 'I love otters,' he said tenderly, cupping the otter in his large hands. 'When I was small we had two cats. The male was called Sam and it always used to sleep curled up next to me. It was **my** cat, **my** friend and it sat on a stool next to me when I ate.' He carefully returned the otter to its place and closed the door of the cabinet. 'After Sam died I discovered that otters had faces like his, the same chubby cheeks and honest eyes,' he continued, 'and I've loved them ever since. I tried to read Tarka the Otter and Ring of Bright Water but they just made me sad. I want to go to the Otter Reserve at Bungay in Suffolk but I never seem to get the time.'

On another shelf was an invitation on crisp, white card. 'The Master of the Household has received Her Majesty's Command to invite Mr Nick Faldo to an evening reception to be given at Buckingham Palace by the Queen and the Duke of Edinburgh on Thursday, 17th May 1984. Dress, uniform for serving officers, black tie. Guests are asked to arrive between 10.00 and 10.15. Replies should be addressed to the Master of the Household, Buckingham Palace.'

Faldo lined up another snooker ball. Crack! It vanished into a pocket. He looked up. 'I was very honoured. There have only been four of these do's in the last twenty-five years and the last was six years ago. The Royals were everywhere. I kept thinking, "What do I do if I walk around a corner and bump into the Queen?" I was much more nervous than I've ever been on a golf course. Then they only went and brought Prince Philip over to meet me, which I thought was a bit strong. I chatted to him for ten minutes about sport and he was great. He made me feel so relaxed. I completely forgot who he was.'

Faldo had been competing in the French Open in Paris that week and had dashed back to London to attend the reception. Flattered as he was at being asked, he was even more flattered by being repeatedly thanked for returning to England. He didn't bump into the Queen as he had feared but he was introduced to her when he was standing with June Croft, the swimmer. 'I felt so tall talking to the Queen I had to stop myself leaning forward. She knew I'd won in America and we talked about that. Then the conversation turned to swimming and I said I used to swim as well. She looked at me and said, "You have lovely broad shoulders."'

The telephone rang and Faldo went to answer it. Cradling a mug of tea in one hand, his girl friend Gill Bennett pointed at the new chintz curtains with their scalloped pelmets that hung over the french windows. 'They're made by a friend who used to do work for the Royals,' she said, a touch of mischief in her voice. I couldn't help smiling. She led the way into the kitchen and poured us each another cup of tea. In the middle of the breakfast bar was a small rectangular raised surface, clearly meant for condiments. 'Nick has just finished grouting these in,' she said, running a finger over the tiles.

Faldo had recently satisfied a long-held ambition and, at one end of the double garage, had built himself a workbench on which he had fitted a big vice and a loft-and-lie machine. He stored his golf shoes underneath the bench in cupboards rescued from the kitchen. He is very good at do-it-yourself and can't help running his finger over a piece of joinery to test the workmanship. In his spare moments he takes the Black and Decker drill Gill gave him for his birthday and attends to minor jobs around the house.

The telephone clicked as the receiver was replaced and Faldo reappeared at the doorway. It was time to go to work. 'Got your tape recorder?' he asked. 'Let's go and get on then.'

This book is the product of that and many other meetings, as well as of my observations gathered from covering golf since the autumn of 1980. It is not a fully-fledged biography. Rather it is an attempt to examine a top-class sportsman approaching the peak years of his sporting life, to find out how he got there, who was influential along the way and how he is setting about trying to reach the summit. And it's on that premise I hope the book will be enjoyed.

CHAPTER 1

HERITAGE –
Triumph in South Carolina

Nick Faldo stood on the edge of the fairway, impassive and motionless, his left hand resting lightly on the rim of his yellow golf bag. Beside him in a blue caddie's smock, dark trousers and scuffed white plimsolls was his caddie Dave McNeilly, whose fair hair was being tugged by a teasing wind. They both stared towards the tiny green.

'How far, Dave?' Faldo asked.

'159 to the flag', McNeilly replied, looking at the yardages he had jotted down in a notebook he now held in his right hand.

Faldo's ball lay on the left of the fairway on this hole, the 15th at Harbour Town on Hilton Head Island, South Carolina, and the 69th hole of the 1984 Sea Pines Heritage Classic. Faldo had hit his second shot across from the right in order to escape from the bunker where his drive had landed. The longer he surveyed his third shot on the 561-yard hole, the more difficult it seemed.

Directly in front of him, cutting into the fairway, was a stand of pine trees, whose tumbling branches were obscuring most of the heavily-bunkered green from Faldo as he stood by his ball. Water ran down the left of the fairway as well. All Faldo could see was a portion of the right side of the green. He walked forward until he was directly under the trees and looked up. 'Can I get over these?' he asked himself, calculating that they were at least 100 feet high.   He returned to his bag and once more looked down the fairway. Picking up some grass and letting it blow from his hand, he noticed with some satisfaction that what wind there was came from the right and behind. After a few moments of deliberation he pulled out a seven iron. As McNeilly lifted the bag and carried it away, Faldo tried to visualise in his mind's eye the shot he wanted to play. He had to start it right of the flag, which was set on the right of the green, to allow for the wind. He had to be sure it went high enough to clear the grasping pine branches. And it had to curl in, otherwise it would end in the bunker on the right of the green. That was his plan, anyway.

It was a crucial shot. Tom Kite, who was playing immediately ahead of Faldo, had pulled back four shots and just drawn level. For the first time for 47 holes Faldo was not in the lead on his own. He had played steadily all day, though less accurately than in his three previous rounds. Now it looked as though he could be overtaken just when he was in sight of his first victory on the US tour. Gil Morgan had finished with a 66 for a total of 274, the same as Ronnie Black, a young American with one tournament victory to his name. If Faldo faltered now he might fall back to join these two.

It was in Faldo's favour that he was ready to meet such a crisis. This was merely another step on the road he had taken when he began playing golf almost exactly thirteen years earlier. How many times in those first years had he pretended he had two shots to win the Open or one putt to defeat Jack Nicklaus? The tournament he wanted to win more than any other was the Open, the oldest and most famous in the world. But for the time being, to win the Heritage would do very nicely. Determined to improve, Faldo practised harder than most players and spent months each year on the demanding US tour, competing against the best. He was branded a loner by his fellow pros on the European tour and called temperamental by the British press and his single-minded devotion to golf had even contributed to the break-up of his marriage. If all this was to have been worth it, he had to prove himself now.

From a few yards down the fairway McNeilly stared intently at his boss, his teeth set firmly. If the shot was crucial for Faldo, it was also important for McNeilly. He was just starting his third season with Faldo and he wanted to win just as badly, not only to gain an extra measure of respect from older, more experienced caddies but also for his own satisfaction. Besides, he knew he'd make money, since he was always paid a proportion of Faldo's winnings. Normally very relaxed, often to be seen with a wide, infectious smile on his face, he was concentrating now as hard as he had ever done. He leant one elbow on the bag, oblivious to the way the label with Faldo's name on it in bold black letters was hanging half off his smock. He willed Faldo to hit a good shot, at the same time praying that the yardage he had given Faldo was correct.

Faldo stepped up to the ball, shuffled his feet into line, bent his knees and swung the club slowly and smoothly. The ball soared from the clubface, rising high above the branches of the pines before it began to curl in towards its target as if being pulled by some unseen hand. It thudded into the green and rolled to within eight feet of the flag. In the television commentary box Tom Weiskopf gasped with admiration. 'I can't tell you how great a shot that was,' said the 1973 Open champion.

Faldo watched the ball until it disappeared behind the trees. As the roars of applause mingled with the shrieks and whistles which rose up around the green he raised his club in his right hand in a salute and slightly self-consciously repaired his divot with the toe of his right shoe. He felt as if he'd received a charge of electricity and he wasn't going to falter now. Minutes later the putt disappeared into the hole and he had regained the lead.

Faldo parred the 16th and arrived at the short 17th knowing it posed a threat. One of the five bogeys he'd had in his previous rounds had come on this 169-yard hole with its tiny, saucer-like green. Faldo's six iron flew over the water, over the 80-yard-long bunker and ended in the heart of the green. He two-putted safely for his three.

The 18th at Harbour Town is a par four, not unlike the 18th at Pebble Beach or the 10th at Turnberry in the way it curves gently to the left and is guarded all the way by the sea. Faldo needed an accurate drive over scrub and marsh to a point, 200 yards or so from the tee where he was standing, where the fairway bulged out like a pot belly. He took his three wood, as he had from this tee all week, knowing that if he hit the ball too far it would roll into the rough and he might have trouble reaching the green. His drive stopped exactly where he wanted it to, in the middle of the fairway.

Approaching his ball Faldo listened for cheers from Kite's group ahead, cheers that would have greeted a birdie by the American. When none came rolling back he knew he remained in the lead. He had a shot of 185 yards to the flag, again over scrub and marsh but this time over a large bunker in front of the green as well. He had no difficulty in establishing his aim for the flag was just to the left of the famous lighthouse at the back of the green.

As he and McNeilly pondered over club selection he felt calm and composed, which was more than could be said for Evonne Cawley (the former Wimbledon champion) and her husband Roger, who live on Hilton Head Island, and Gill Bennett, Faldo's girl-friend. The three of them were standing together by the green, looking back down the fairway. 'Now I know what it's like to be behind the ropes,' muttered Cawley.

'This is more exciting than Wimbledon.' She stood on tiptoe to peer over the shoulders of two men who had moved in front of her and were blocking her view. 'Come on Nicky,' she said quietly.

Faldo chose a six iron. From the moment he hit the ball it didn't veer from its target, landing just past the flag and bounding over the back of the sloping green, coming to rest two feet short of a bunker and 18 feet from the hole. Faldo had to get the ball from its bare lie and through a collar of light rough that fringed the green before it could reach the putting surface. Using his putter, the most trustworthy of his clubs all week, he rolled the ball to within four inches, a shot that drew almost as much praise from television commentator Ken Venturi as Faldo's shot on the 15th had from Weiskopf. 'He made a good roll. What a good roll! What a good roll! What a great roll that was!' said Venturi, his voice rising in appreciation each time. Kite seated nearby smiled ruefully as Faldo holed. Victory was worth $72,000, but even more than that in self-respect.

Faldo's feelings were of huge excitement which was almost immediately supplanted by relief. He'd been waiting for this victory for a long time. He'd been going to the US for a few months each year since January 1981 and he felt that at last he had made a significant step forward in his climb towards a major championship. Gifted though he was, Faldo was not one of a tiny group of golfers who are so gifted that they can succeed as professionals as soon as they leave the amateur ranks. Jack Nicklaus was one who could, as he had shown by winning the US Open a mere seven months after turning pro. Another was Seve Ballesteros who had burst upon the world as a swaggering, seemingly nerveless teenager when he had tied with Nicklaus for second place in the 1976 Open at Royal Birkdale. Others, like Faldo, Hale Irwin and Tom Watson, had had to serve their apprenticeships by going close to victory in major events before they had

acquired the necessary carapace of confidence and knowledge to win. Faldo had done a lot of winning in Europe – five
tournaments in the previous season alone – but he had also
known the harrowing experiences of being in contention
over the closing holes of a major event only to fall back. He
had done it first at Birkdale in the 1983 Open. The second time
was in the 1984 US Masters just a week before this victory.

Faldo had begun the last round at Augusta National lying
in third place with Ben Crenshaw and David Graham. They
were seven under par. It was the nearest a British player had
been to victory for a decade. But as Crenshaw strode purpose-
fully towards an extremely popular victory, his first in a major
championship after five times finishing runner-up, Faldo had
made four crucial errors on the outward half and had taken 40
strokes to reach the 10th tee. His 76 had dropped him to joint
15th.

For Gill Bennett, watching Faldo play so badly had been
an unprecedented experience. A vivacious brunette, who
seemed to be dwarfed whenever she stood next to Faldo, she
had arrived from England in January and when news of her
presence leaked out it prompted Faldo's wife Melanie, at
home in Hertfordshire, to begin divorce proceedings.

Gill knew little about golf, other than what she had
been able to pick up in the six months she had spent in the
London office of International Management Group, Mark
McCormack's firm. She was secretary to John Simpson,
Faldo's manager and closest friend, and had first met Faldo
during the Open at Birkdale in 1983. Gill liked sport but had
never touched a golf club and so she usually carried a score
card of each course as she walked around and often she
jotted down notes as an **aide-mémoire**.

Perhaps she was a talisman for Faldo, for since arriving in
the US she had followed every one of his rounds and seen
him go from strength to strength. On this occasion, the last
day at Augusta, she had been deeply affected by watching

the world of someone she cared for fall apart in front of her eyes. When she had reached the ninth green she had been torn. 'I wanted to walk into the clubhouse, to burst into tears, to go and hide. In fact do anything but watch,' she said later. 'But I knew in my heart of hearts that I had to stay with Nick. I knew I must support him in bad times as well as good.'

Faldo had been disappointed but not distraught about this performance. In their hotel room that night he had consoled Gill by saying, 'Don't get too upset. You may have worse times than that. But you'll also have better times. What has happened has happened. There is no point in worrying about it.'

Nevertheless Faldo was pondering on it on Monday April 16th as he drove north-east from Georgia to South Carolina. He decided to change his attitude. At the Heritage he would go for everything, long putts and all. It was to be his last tournament in the US for some weeks so the worst that could happen would be for him to miss the cut and have to fly back to London early. He remembers thinking to himself, 'It's either going to go very right or very wrong,' and not particularly caring one way or the other. Immediately a weight was lifted from his shoulders and he relaxed a little more.

In keeping with this apparently carefree new attitude he also decided to practise less than usual. He had worked hard for weeks. If ever he was in credit, it was now. Before the tournament he hit no more than 100 balls each day, including chipping practice. He would throw balls into impossible situations in bunkers and flop them out casually, indolently almost. After dinner each night, when the sun had gone down and the mosquitoes disappeared, he would take his putter and two or three balls and cross the road from the condominium where he and Gill were staying to do some serious putting practice. Sometimes McNeilly would be there as well.

Since he had started working for Faldo in the spring of

1982, McNeilly had established a relationship with his boss that was stronger than most caddies have with their employers. He was one of a new breed, young men who were often good players themselves, but not good enough to cut the mustard as pros. These men were a far cry from the traditional type of caddie, the veteran wanderers, Knights of the Road, men with tattooed forearms who drank a good few pints as often as they could afford to. McNeilly himself had attended North East London Polytechnic, where he did a degree course in French, psychology and economics. 'Three blissful years and at the end of it I got a BA General – failed,' was his endearingly honest way of describing his days as a student.

The ambitious Englishman and the thirty-three-year-old Ulsterman, who gave the appearance of being as carefree as a cloud, complemented one another. McNeilly could be casual to the point of indifference and when he was then Faldo, who is driven by a burning ambition in matters to do with golf, wouldn't hesitate to pull him back into line. Yet when Faldo became too tense for his own good McNeilly had the knack of introducing the apposite comment. Now he produced a gem, apt and barbed. 'Nick,' he said to Faldo on the putting green, 'if we're going back at the end of the week I think we've left it a little late for our first win over here.'

Faldo, McNeilly's comment ringing in his ears, played beautifully on the first day. As early as the second hole, a par five, he had an opportunity to test his new philosophy when he faced a 40-foot putt. Instead of trying to get it close he went for it and duly sank it, just as he did another birdie putt on the next hole and yet another on the long fifth. He might have faltered on the eighth when he was faced with a testing second shot to a green with a lake on the left. Faldo has a tendency to drag the ball left. This time though, his four iron reached the fringe and he walked up to it nonchalantly, thinking 'I'll hole this. That would be good wouldn't it?' This putt went in and so did two more for birdies on the inward half, and without really knowing what had been going on Faldo was leading the tournament. His five under par 66 remained the day's best until it was overtaken by Gil Morgan's 64 in the late afternoon. Tom Watson, the defending champion, and Tom Kite were among those on 68.

After his round Faldo was hitting a few practice putts when his former caddie, Andy Prodger, ambled over. Prodger, a small, muscular man with black curly hair and a rolling, seaman's walk, had been Faldo's second caddie. They lasted together for two seasons until they fell out, neither being able to communicate with the other. 'What's all this about the nickname you were given by some British newspapers after the Masters?' asked Prodger. Faldo looked up, startled. At this moment he didn't know he had been described as 'El Foldo.' 'They reckoned you folded on Sunday,' said Prodger. Faldo carried on putting, biting his lip and banging the balls towards the hole with evident frustration.

This was the culmination of an uneasy relationship, dating back to 1979, Faldo's first unsuccessful year, with some of the British press. He had behaved badly then, to such an extent that Gerald Micklem, one of his most loyal supporters, had ticked him off in a letter, and press support for the former golden boy had begun to wane. It became not unusual to see him described as sullen, spoiled or surly. He was cast as the anti-hero and his contemporary, Sandy Lyle, was seen as the epitome of the British hero – easy-going, affable, and straight-forward, making everything seem easy without appearing to try too hard. Newspapers liked to remind their readers that Faldo had once reported Lyle, alleging that he had contra-vened the rules by sticking tape on his putter to stop the glare of the sun. Faldo's allegation was later upheld by the tournament director. In the Lyle-Faldo relationship, and the way it was described in the press, there was more than an echo of the relationship between Steve Ovett and Sebastian Coe and the press.

Faldo could not understand that if he talked to a journalist for half an hour about half a dozen different subjects he might be quoted on only one or two of those subjects. To him this seemed to be misrepresentation. An example was to occur at the US PGA tournament in 1984 when a local reporter interviewed Faldo the day he arrived in Shoal Creek and they talked widely for forty-five minutes.

'As soon as they ask me a question I have to sift through my mind to think what's he trying to get out of this, what slant is he trying to put on it?' Faldo said of British journalists in this interview. 'So you can't be open, free, natural, because there will be a stupid headline the next day which will make you look big-headed, stupid.' He went on to say that stories were sensationalised, twisted in order to sell newspapers and that he was often misquoted. 'They quote you out of character [context] and then add a couple of words to your quote to make it more exciting.'

Faldo later confirmed that this story accurately reported what he had said, but then pointed out that he had talked about other aspects of his life as well – his aims and ambitions, his views about the US tour, the rising standard of European golf – and why hadn't all that been mentioned? He couldn't have criticised the headline though. It read: 'Faldo takes a swing at British press'.

Golf was – and remains – the most important thing in Faldo's life and when it went wrong he became very intense about it and unwilling to accommodate journalists and their deadlines. He considered refusing interviews, but was talked out of that by Simpson, who explained that all that would do would be to make him appear aloof. He thought about not reading the papers and magazines, but decided against that since he was always told what was in them anyway.

When Faldo heard about the El Foldo story he was betwixt and between in his relationship with the British press. He had mellowed a little towards them after his marvellous year in

Europe in 1983, when he had won five tournaments in all, three of them consecutively. On the other hand he couldn't forget the way he and Gill had been hounded for days after the news of his leaving Melanie had broken in January.

Goaded by thoughts of El Foldo, Faldo birdied the second hole of the second round to overtake Morgan. He was not to lose the lead again. He birdied the third by holing a good putt and the long fifth by reaching it in two. He had now broken clear of the rest of the field and his only moments of worry came when he was bunkered on the eleventh and twelfth and forfeited shots on each hole. He regained them immediately with good putts: from 25 feet on the 13th and 12 feet on the par three 14th. A 67 gave him a halfway total of 133, nine under par, which was two strokes ahead of Tom Kite. Gil Morgan had faded with a 73, the same score as Tom Watson's.

At the start of the third round of a golf tournament the leader must pick his way past the ghosts of men who have been out in front and then disappeared – men like Tom Watson at Medinah in the 1975 US Open and Bobby Clampett in the 1982 Open at Royal Troon. Though Faldo's total was the same as Clampett's had been, he had no intention of collapsing. He was a hardened veteran compared with Clampett, who had been only three months past his twenty-second birthday and in only his third season as a pro when he had taken Scotland by storm. Faldo, at twenty-six, was three years older, had been a pro for eight years and knew what it felt like to win tournaments.

'One of the old caddies said years ago that we in Europe have got something over the guys in America,' says Faldo. 'We've won tournaments, whereas many of them have not. When you're coming down the stretch winning is winning. It's the same tightening of the stomach muscles, the same bursts of adrenalin, whether you're about to win £8,000 in Europe or $80,000 in the States. You've had it before and coped with it and won, whereas a lot of these guys are looking for their first wins. They might not have had the feeling of victory since their college days.'

Faldo's new approach was working and all round his play was solid – his driving was straight, his chipping good, his putting spectacular. He relished the different texture of Harbour Town's Bermuda-grassed greens compared with the lightning-fast greens sown with bent grass at Augusta. He found that his Ping Pal putter, with which he had won those European tournaments in 1983, felt much more comfortable than had his Daiwa putter at Augusta. And if Faldo showed any signs of faltering, then his caddy was there ready to use a little psychology. Once when McNeilly wanted a little extra he handed over the required club and said, 'Now Mr Faldo, I want something special this time,' slowly and deliberately emphasising the Mr and the first syllable of Faldo's surname. The message was clear. 'I had never called Nick Mr Faldo before, but he knew what I was talking about,' says McNeilly. 'It was like a kick in the backside for him.'

All week Faldo had started brilliantly and he did so again when playing with Kite and Black on Saturday. This was just as well because in the breathless calm that hung over the course Denis Watson, the South African, equalled Jack Nicklaus's course record of 63. Faldo's response was three birdies in the first five holes: a drive and a smooth six iron to six feet at the first, two woods and a chip to five feet at the second and a successful scramble for a four on the fifth, when he got down in a chip and a putt. At the ninth his tee shot ended in an evil little bunker. 'Just like a little pot bunker back home,' Faldo thought as he looked at his lie. He was 12 feet from the hole and four or five feet beneath it. His explosion shot finished close enough for him to sink the putt, and he remembers thinking that if he could get up and down from there he could get up and down from anywhere. Apart from bunkering his seven iron tee shot at the short 17th, which cost him a shot, he played steadily to the end and finished in 69, four shots ahead of Kite.

Four shots is quite a cushion, but as he lay in bed that night Faldo felt the first twinges of anxiety. The words 'El Foldo' danced before his eyes and he thought of other comments that had been made about his alleged weakness under pressure. It subsequently turned out that no British paper had referred to him as El Foldo but, unaware of this, Faldo was still smarting about it and that very afternoon he had a confrontation with David Davies of the **Guardian**, the only British golf correspondent at the tournament. But what if he were to lose? He would have thrown away a substantial lead and those cutting jibes would be seen to have been correct after all.

With hindsight it is clear that he had less to worry about than he might have thought. He had only to consider his record in the US for a moment or two to realise that he was due for his first victory. His improvement since he first arrived in 1981 had been steady – joint eighth (Glen Campbell Los Angeles Open 1981), joint seventh (Hawaiian Open 1982), joint fifth (Canadian Open 1982) and outright third place in the Greater Greensboro Open in 1981.

Then in the Ryder Cup in the autumn of 1983 Faldo's striking had been so crisp and authoritative that no one could have doubted that he was capable of winning a tournament in America. Indeed, a week later he had very nearly done just that. While his team-mates returned to Heathrow on board Concorde, Faldo had driven to Orlando to compete in the Walt Disney World Golf Classic. He had needed several thousand dollars to retain his player's card, his passport to the US circuit, and far from nervously grinding out four safe rounds he had gone for glory from the start. With a blazing last round of 66, six under par, he had tied for second place with Mark McCumber, two strokes behind the winner Payne Stewart. The $35,200 Faldo had won easily guaranteed his exemption from having to pre-qualify for tournaments in

1984. Maybe that had taken a weight off his mind for in the early events of 1984, the events preceding the Heritage, Faldo had played better than ever before in the US. Three times in seven weeks he had finished in the top ten.

Had he been so inclined Faldo could have ticked off all those performances by way of reassurance. He could even have taken consolation from another feature of the American tour, the increasing success of non-Americans. The best example was Seve Ballesteros, who had plundered the rich pickings to such effect in 1983, winning two of the eight tournaments he had entered and taking $150,000 in prize money home to Spain.

In fact, foreign players had won, or finished runners-up, in more than one quarter of the forty-two tournaments.

But Faldo ignored these portents and worked out his own reasons. 'You led all day Saturday, what's so different now?' he asked as he busied himself around the condominium before the final round. 'It's not as if you're leading for the first time. Gosh! panic! You've led this lot since the 20th hole. Now go out and play good.'

And play good is just what he did, after receiving a kindly pat on the shoulder and a 'You can do it Nick,' from Hubert Green while they were both practising their putting. He birdied the first, again. 'That'll show 'em I mean business,' he thought, glancing at his playing partners Larry Rinker and Dan Pohl as they all walked to the second tee. Then he reeled off eight pars, saving himself with another marvellous bunker shot from a plugged lie on the seventh. He had to put one foot in the bunker and one foot out of it to play this shot. He wasn't so accurate with his shots into the green as in earlier rounds and he twice had to save par with deft pitches. His outward half of 35 was the highest of the week. Kite, meanwhile, had lopped two strokes from Faldo's overnight lead, going out in 33 and then birdieing the 12th and 13th to draw level.

Faldo, playing behind, heard the cheers indicating that Kite had caught him. He determined to continue to be aggressive. McNeilly handed him an eight iron on the 14th tee and said, 'Just swing it slow and hit it right at the stick.' The ball landed 15 feet from the flag but Faldo missed the putt. Everything was now beginning to take its toll: the wind of the first two days, and the relentless pressure of leading a high-class field over a stern golf course. It was a help that Evonne Cawley was there, shouting out, 'Well done Nicky!' every time he hit a good shot, and that there were several groups of British supporters in his gallery, some of whom were carrying a Union Jack. Still, he knew he'd missed one chance with that putt and he wasn't completely relaxed by McNeilly's consoling whisper, 'Just hit them close, Nick. We'll make one sooner or later.'

And so Faldo arrived at the 15th, the edge of the precipice. Had he faltered then he might never have recovered. He might have been like Ed Sneed in the 1979 Masters. Sneed had been leading by three shots after 15 holes of the last round. As he had walked to the 16th tee he had been thinking to himself, 'It's impossible not to win.' Those words had so tempted the gods that they had made him squander shots at each of the last three holes so that he had tied with Tom Watson and Fuzzy Zoeller. After such a collapse, Sneed had been in no mood to fight out a play-off and Zoeller had taken the green jacket – traditionally awarded to the winner of the Masters – on the second extra hole. Sneed did win another tournament eventually, but his name and that year's Masters are inextricably bound together. The 1979 Masters is known as 'Sneed's Masters'.

But as we have seen, Faldo looked over the precipice and did not fall. The fortitude he showed that afternoon marked him out as being one of a select breed – a man capable of winning one of golf's four major championships and thereby becoming Britain's first truly world-class golfer since Tony

Jacklin a decade or more earlier. Who knows, he might yet become as much of a sporting hero as Jacklin or even Jacklin's predecessor, the great Henry Cotton.

To those of us back home the news of Faldo's triumph seemed an age in coming. Surely it hadn't even taken this long to take the good news from Ghent to Aix? George and Joyce Faldo were staying at a cottage near Holt in Norfolk over Easter and just before midday on Easter Sunday they walked into the village to buy the papers. The only stories from the Heritage were those after Friday's second round. 'Never mind the second round,' they thought to themselves. 'What about yesterday's round? And today's for that matter.'

John Simpson was spending the holiday week-end at Gleneagles with his wife Jane and their eighteen-month old baby Benjamin. On Saturday evening he had spoken to Faldo on the telephone and on Sunday afternoon, while playing a round of golf himself, he kept thinking about events across the Atlantic. His sense of business told him that if Faldo won it would mean at least another £100,000 from contract bonuses and appearance money, in addition to the prize money. Victory would also be the next step in the progression that the two of them had both hoped for.

First would come the titles in Europe, then a tournament in the States, and finally success in a major, either the Masters, US Open, the Open or the US PGA.

At the cottage that Sunday evening Joyce Faldo drew the curtains when dusk came. She scoured the paper and found there would be a late night news bulletin preceded by a programme of organ music. She twiddled with the dial of the small portable radio until strident organ music filled the room. The news was dominated by Easter messages from the Pope and the Archbishop of Canterbury. There was a brief mention of the miners' strike that had begun the month before. After ten minutes Joyce Faldo was beside herself, shaking and almost physically sick with worry. Her heart sank when the ringing tones of the announcer said, 'That is the end of the news.' Then he added, 'For golf enthusiasts there is good news.' His voice was drowned as Joyce Faldo let out a shriek of excitement. 'Thank God!' she cried. 'Nick must be so thrilled.'

A few hours later Simpson was woken by the telephone. He hadn't heard the news and, heavy with sleep, he wasn't quite sure what was happening until he heard Faldo's excited voice shouting down the line, 'I've done it, John! I've done it! I beat Kite by one shot!'

Faldo's rounds of 66, 67, 68, 69 totalled 270, 14 under par, and equalled the tournament record Tom Watson had set in 1979. Those 270 strokes comprised 19 birdies, five bogeys, 48 pars. Faldo hit 49 greens in regulation (13 in the first and third rounds, 12 in the second and 11 in the last) and took 110 putts (27, 28, 28 and 27 respectively) on the four days.

If a person reveals his character by the books he reads then a golfer can be judged by the quality of the courses on which he wins tournaments. Harbour Town was designed by Pete Dye with assistance from Jack Nicklaus and opened in the late nineteen sixties. Since then it has become one of the thirty leading courses in the US and those who have won there include Arnold Palmer, Hale Irwin, Johnny Miller, Hubert Green, Tom Watson, Bill Rogers and Fuzzy Zoeller. In fact, only two winners of this tournament, prior to Faldo, have not won a major championship. Clearly Faldo was moving into illustrious company.

Soon telegrams and letters were on their way, from Henry Cotton in Penina, Peter Alliss in Hindhead, Tony and Vivien Jacklin in Spain, Deane Beman at the headquarters of the American PGA tour, Bernard and Lesley Gallacher at Wentworth, and Ken Schofield of the European Tour Players' Division. Two British families, visiting the US on holiday, wrote and congratulated Faldo 'for making them feel proud to be British'.

The evening passed in a cloud of celebrations, first at 'Evonne's', the Cawleys' nightclub, and then back at their house. The first fingers of light were stretching across the sky when Faldo decided to end the celebrations. His elation had been replaced by a warm glow, a feeling of satisfaction at a job done well. Now there could be no more El Foldo. Facing the greatest crisis of his life he had delivered the goods spectacularly. That seven-iron shot of his had won him the tournament as surely as Watson's chip-in gave him the 1982 US Open, as Sarazen's albatross on the 15th at Augusta gave him the 1935 Masters. In his own mind Faldo hoped that everyone who saw this seven-iron shot would enthuse about it as they did about Jones's bunker shot at Royal Lytham in 1926 and Trevino's chip-in on the 71st hole at Muirfield in the 1972 Open. Of all the millions of shots hit during thousands of hours of golf this one was, quite simply, the greatest shot Nick Faldo had ever played.

CHAPTER 2

The Important Counsellors

Now that our champion has been crowned, has become the first Briton to win a tournament on American soil since Tony Jacklin in 1972, it is time to pause and examine him more closely. Perhaps I should begin by saying how I became interested in Nick Faldo and why I wanted to write a book about him rather than, say, Bernhard Langer, Sam Torrance, Greg Norman or Sandy Lyle.

In the autumn of 1980 I changed from rugby correspondent of the **Sunday Times** to become golf correspondent, a position previously held with great distinction by the late Henry Longhurst. Moving from one sport to another I was struck by a number of differences between Britain's second winter sport and its second summer sport. Rugby was still amateur in that the players had jobs to go to on Monday morning. Golf was very professional, a way of life for the participants.

Rugby was essentially a static spectator's sport lasting eighty minutes and all the journalists were seated together, like judges at an ice-dancing contest, while the game unfolded in front of us. Happily, the players never felt they were performing **for** us despite having to play **in front of** us. A golf tournament by contrast is diffuse. It lasts four days, involves more than 100 players, always produces a winner (there are few draws in golf) and the action is spread over 100 acres from seven in the morning to seven at night. If rugby has its thud and blunder, then golf is not without an element of blood and thunder.

An essential part of the fabric of rugby was that which took place in the clubhouse after a match. I soon discovered that once a golf pro has concluded his round, been interviewed by the media and finished practising for the day, he has had enough. His day at the office is over: now he is entitled to some time on his own.

One of the most vivid impressions I retain from my days as a neophyte golf correspondent is of the intensity with which the pros applied themselves. I was used to the roar and shrill peep of a track-suited coach and his whistle. Golf pros didn't need a coach to spur them on. They all had their routines: an hour's warm-up, which would end with fifteen minutes putting. Then they would march briskly to the first tee, shrugging away autograph hunters, while their caddies struggled behind, listing slightly under the weight of golf bags that were large enough to carry twice as many as the statutory fourteen clubs. They played their round, often with little visible pleasure, signed their card and disappeared. Some would return later and head for the practice ground or putting green and Faldo, I noticed, seemed always to be one of the last to leave.

I also found out quite soon that he was a loner. I liked that. There were not many loners in rugby. He was described to me as being temperamental. Other journalists talked of tantrums and of him not always cooperating with them. I half expected them to tap the sides of their noses and wink when they said this, as if they were imparting some secret tenet of free-masonry. I was intrigued. Did we have a winner here? Was Faldo a man who wanted to win more than he wanted to be graceful in coming second?

I searched him out and, as I got to know him, discovered

that at the age of fourteen he and I had played golf to a similar standard. This surprised me. I had imagined that a professional golfer would not only have had to have started playing very young, in the same way as a swimmer or an athlete does, but that he would also have become very good very young. I once was given a golf lesson by a pro who had been scratch when he was fourteen. I looked through my golf books and found I was right in thinking that Faldo had taken up the game comparatively late. By their fourteenth birthdays, Jack Nicklaus had broken 70 on a championship course, Bernhard Langer was less than a year from turning pro, Seve Ballesteros had been playing for seven years and Sandy Lyle, after first gripping a club when he was two, was winning monthly medals at his father's club and about to become a boy international.

Spending more time with Faldo I learned of other traits we had in common. Neither of us had performed with any distinction at school; we had both spent time in the US when we were in our late teens. My interest was caught. I began watching him closely when he played and I also discovered that he was a man influenced by only a few people. I suggest that half a dozen people, no more, helped him to become good enough to win the Heritage in 1984. These people were his early influences.

Behind every successful man is a woman and the woman behind many a successful sportsman frequently is his mother. Tennis players Rod Laver and Jimmy Connors are only children of mothers who were highly ambitious for them and each has borne out Freud's notion that 'a man who has been the undisputed favourite of his mother keeps for life the feeling of being a conqueror, that confidence of success which often induces real success'. So, too, has Nick Faldo, who is the only child of George and Joyce Faldo, and very much the product of his mother's influence.

Joyce Faldo is a tall, warm-hearted lady with high cheekbones and brown eyes. She was born in Knella Road, Welwyn Garden City, the road where later she and George would live and where their son Nicholas Faldo would be born. If asked why she had only one child she will explain that she and her husband were both very influenced by the struggles their parents went through in the thirties. Money was short during their childhood and it has left them both with a natural cautiousness in financial matters. George Faldo's upbringing furthermore was quite a tough one. He had four brothers and sisters and they all lived with their parents in the East End of London in a flat that had no running water and a lavatory that had to be shared with neighbours. Just before the Second World War one of George's brothers died of food poisoning.

In 1957 the Faldos were living in a two-bedroomed council house in Knella Road. Joyce, who was clever with her hands, was working as a cutter and pattern drafter for Cresta Silks; George had just begun work in the financial planning department of ICI Plastics. They had been married for ten years when, at three o'clock in the afternoon on Thursday July 18, Joyce gave birth to a son, whom they later christened Nicholas Alexander. He weighed seven pounds twelve ounces and, seeing how long and skinny he was, the midwife in attendance forecast he would grow to be six feet two inches tall. It was an accurate forecast; he is six feet three inches.

Nick had a happy childhood in which any shortage of money was more than made up for by the care and attention lavished on him. The family's financial precepts were laid down by George, probably influenced by his parents. 'I always said that if we had a roof over our heads and enough food and heat then we were okay. We certainly didn't believe in having anything we could not put up the money for, apart from a mortgage.'

Both parents enjoyed occasional visits to the theatre and to Gilbert and Sullivan operettas, and more than once George played an uproarious Widow Twankey in an amateur production of **Aladdin.** On Saturday mornings they would take Nick and drive to the Festival Hall, London, to attend an Ernest Read concert for children. Each Boxing Day there was a family outing to a pantomime, cinema or theatre.

A brother of George's had a caravan at Sheringham, Norfolk, and they spent many holidays there. Nick's bike would be the first thing to be unloaded from the roof of the car and he would be off exploring the lanes of Norfolk, only returning in time for food. Several summers were spent camping in France, in the Loire valley and near Paris.

At eight or nine Faldo's headmaster told his parents, 'I don't know what he is going to do when he grows up but I'm certain he'll do it well.' After that Nick's childhood was carefully planned by his mother. 'First we wanted him to be an actor,' she remembers. 'We thought he'd be another Sir Laurence Olivier. We took him to dancing and elocution lessons. We tried to interest him in music. We knew he'd win the Tchaikovsky piano prize. He had smashing legs and I wanted him to be a model so I used to take him to Harrods fashion shows. Finally, we realised he was only interested in sport.'

Their son was physically and mentally well equipped to be a sportsman. He was tall and long-legged, like his father, and he had excellent hand-eye coordination. Most of all, he had a burning desire to win. He was never any good in team events at school because he could not understand why some of his team-mates took sport less seriously than he did, but he was brilliant at individual sports. At ten, he was the Hertfordshire under-eleven 100-metres breaststroke champion. For a while he had tennis lessons and his parents bought him a handsome racquet. He tried canoeing, even building his own canoe, and then cycling. He had a bike for road racing and another for track racing, which he did with the Welwyn Wheelers at a banked circuit near his parents' house.

When he was eleven a friend examined his handwriting

and reported that, among other things, he was 'subjective but has a great desire to achieve greatness', was 'clear-minded, strongly egoistic' and showed 'a lack of modesty and a tendency to loneliness'. By now he was big and strong enough to outwrestle his father in the friendly brawls they had on the sitting room floor. The student daughter of a friend of George's sister lived with them for a year and noted Nick's burgeoning temper when he had been defeated, a temper that amused his parents. 'We'd hear the gate go boing, boing, boing and then the bike would be thrown aside and we'd laugh to ourselves,' says his father. 'We were with him if he'd lost. We were sympathetic. There's no point in playing games if you're not going to try to win.' In the family these tantrums were known as Nick's Maria Callases.

There were not many sports that Nick hadn't tried by the time he was a teenager, but one was golf. He wasn't to remain unfamiliar with it much longer. At Easter in 1971 Faldo was watching his parents' new colour television when shots of Jack Nicklaus playing in the Masters at Augusta were transmitted. He leaned forward in his seat, entranced. It all looked so beautiful. Those same Easter holidays he received his first golf lesson, booked for him by his mother, and a few months later his parents gave him a half set of golf clubs costing thirty-six pounds for his fourteenth birthday.

His golf development so far falls neatly between the scratchy experiences of Seve Ballesteros and the cosseted upbringing of Jack Nicklaus. As a seven-year-old Ballesteros fashioned his first club from the head of a three iron he had been given, to which he attached a stick found in a field. By soaking the club in water overnight the shaft would swell and fit snugly into the hosel. Ballesteros scoured the beach at Pedrena for pebbles that doubled as golf balls and the first holes he played were marked out on the beach or in the dirt at his parents' farm.

Nicklaus, on the other hand, came from a prosperous,

middle-class family that was rich enough to afford a maid. When Jack took up golf, aged ten, he was immediately given a set of clubs that had been specially cut down. He was also fortunate in being able to play over an outstanding course, Scioto Country Club, a course designed by the great Donald Ross and good enough to have been the site of the 1926 US Open, won by Bobby Jones. As far as his golf was concerned, Nicklaus never wanted for anything for longer than it took him to sign a chit, which would be presented to his father at the end of each month.

What was uniquely Faldo's was a total lack of the sort of parental or family guidance that Ballesteros had from his older brothers and his uncle Ramon Sota, the distinguished Spanish pro, and Jack Nicklaus received from his father Charlie.

Just before his sixteenth birthday, Faldo left school, to all intents and purposes to play golf. Though he had a handful of O levels and CSE's – metalwork and woodwork, English, maths and technical drawing – his real qualifications were at golf. Nothing else interested him. 'I totally lost interest in school from the age of fifteen', says Faldo. 'I just couldn't see any way in which an algebraic equation was going to help me with my golf.' His parents assumed that he would become an assistant pro and visited the local library to look at job advertisements in the golf magazines. 'I wasn't worried about Nick,' his mother recalls. 'I had complete faith in his ability. Besides, George and I were reassured by what everyone said about his golf. Wherever I took him to compete in junior competitions, local golf experts used to come up to me and pour praise on Nick's head. I felt he was bound to succeed.'

For a time thereafter Faldo would while away each day in the same manner. First thing in the morning he would fasten his clubs on to his bicycle and strap a round tupperware lunch box on the handlebars. His lunch hardly ever varied: cheddar cheese and salad cream sandwiches or pickles, cheese and

salad cream sandwiches which had become curved by
lunchtime as a result of being packed around the edge of his
lunch box; yoghurt; an orange; an apple; a Penguin chocolate
biscuit and a chunk of cooking dates. He would cycle to the
golf club and practise until it was dark.

With his sportsman's eye for a ball and his excellent rhythm
Faldo learned the complex patterns and disciplines of golf
very quickly. Stretching his parents' modest finances, he had
an average of one lesson a week for two years, the first costing
only fifty pence. 'I can still remember the first time I gave him a
lesson,' says Ian Connelly, who was professional at Welwyn
Garden City Golf Club at that time. 'It wasn't so much that he
had talent, because a lot of kids have talent. Nick had
something else as well – ambition. There are plenty of kids
with talent but there aren't that many with talent **and** a
burning ambition.'

By now it was clear that Faldo loved golf to the exclusion of
everything else. He showed no interest in girls nor in going to
discos. He wasn't concerned about football, other than to ask
his father on a Saturday night how Leeds United had fared.
His life was dominated by golf, as Tony Jacklin's had been at
the same age ten or twelve years earlier. Faldo relished the
fact that golf was a game he could play by himself. All he had
to do was to climb on his bike, cycle to the golf club and there
he found a contentment he had never experienced at any
other sport and most certainly not at school.

Faldo loved practising and he did it winter and summer,
good weather and bad. Using balls he had found by
rummaging through the bushes that separated the 9th and
10th fairways, he practised until his hands bled. Hardly a
week passed but that he needed a new glove, some new
shoes, waterproofs, new clubs even. His mother would drive
him wherever he wanted to go, once as far as Guildford for a
boys' county match when the other passenger was Ken
Brown, and on another occasion to Woodhall Spa in

Lincolnshire. No one doubted that all this hard work was paying off.

Less than four years after first touching a club he was selected to play in a very strong English boys' team against the Scots. His team-mates at Hoylake included Paul Hoad, Sandy Lyle and Brown. Faldo lost both his matches, but much more important in the long term was the fact that he came under the scrutiny of Gerald Micklem.

Micklem is one of the great statesmen of world golf. Possessed of a sharp, though sometimes rheumy, eye and a keen brain, he has dominated amateur golf as an administrator since he stopped playing competitively in the mid fifties. He has an encyclopaedic knowledge of golf and once said that he could find a mistake on each of the 400-odd pages of the **Golfers' Handbook.** Now approaching his ninth decade, he is held in as much reverence at both the Royal and Ancient Golf Club at St Andrews and at Sunningdale as the Earl of Stockton (formerly Harold Macmillan) is among the members of the Tory party. Micklem was not particularly impressed by the Faldo he saw at Hoylake that August.

He was still able to recall the impression made on him ten years earlier by a waif-like boy from the same county as Faldo. 'Peter Townsend was a tremendously good player,' says Micklem. 'He won the Boys' championship when he was fiifteen and again when he was seventeen. He was tiny, very, very small and he had a short game that was out of this world. I think he was one of the best boy players I've ever seen.' Sandy Lyle, who had first played for England Boys' as a fourteen-year-old, was also more impressive than Faldo at that time.

Over the winter of 1974/75 Faldo practised harder than ever. To raise money he sometimes did a day's work laying carpets for a friend, for which he was paid two pounds each day. When he was not working he practised almost every day, even when everything was frozen so hard that his club would ricochet off the ground. He would take a bag of balls and a five iron and say to himself, 'I'm not going to miss the green with any of these.' Once he overheard Connelly and an assistant talking about the punched wedge. Realising he didn't know how to hit such a shot he spent hours hitting wedges into the wind until he had learned how to keep the balls at waist height. Another time he remembers Connelly saying how Christy O'Connor had once stood on the Postage Stamp hole at Troon and hit the green with every club in his bag. That spurred Faldo on and he spent hours learning to hit a two iron 120 yards, a six iron no more than eighty yards.

Early in 1975 Faldo competed in the West of England Open, an amateur strokeplay event held at Saunton in Devon. Micklem was there, watching, and could scarcely believe his eyes when he saw how much Faldo had improved in the intervening six months.

'Something tremendous had happened,' recalls Micklem also remembering how he had rushed off in search of Michael Bonallack. When he found the famous amateur, who was by then reaching the end of his career, he had gushed, 'Michael, I've just seen the best player I've seen for ages and ages. He is terrific. You must play with him.'

During the summer of that year Faldo proved that Micklem's earlier enthusiasm had been well-founded. He swept through one amateur competition after another as no amateur had done in living memory. In a few golden months he won at least eleven events. An example of his rapid improvement is that at the start of the season his handicap of three was too high for him to enter the Lytham Trophy; by the end he was down to plus one. In the English Amateur he became the youngest-ever champion. When he defeated David Ecclestone by 6 and 4 in the 36-hole final at Lytham he was eight days past his eighteenth birthday and it was four years and eight days since he had been given his first clubs.

One of the first to congratulate him was Gerald Micklem

who, shooting stick in hand, had followed the match all day. He and Faldo had come to respect and like one another, their friendship and love for golf bridging the considerable differences in their backgrounds and ages. 'I always listened to Gerald because he presented things so well,' says Faldo. 'I remember I threw my clubs down in disgust somewhere and he came up to me later and said, "I've just got to chat to you. I didn't like you throwing your clubs down like that. I used to do it and you can see that it never got me anywhere." He didn't say to me: 'If I ever see you doing that again I'll . . ." He said "I used to do that," and I appreciated it. I realised I wasn't the only one. At that time in my career he was the only person, apart from Ian Connelly, who if he said something to me I knew he was saying it for my own good. As a result I would try my darndest to do whatever he suggested.

'He spoke such good sense,' Faldo continued. 'It was straight to the point. He never wasted words. He would tell me what I had to do or what had gone wrong and then leave me to decide how to cope with it. I can hear him now saying to me in that distinctive way he has, "I'll leave you to work out what the best solution is for that." '

From September until December Faldo practised every bit as hard by day as he had in the same period the previous year. By night he fended away offers of golf scholarships to American universities. David Williams, coach of the highly successful University of Houston golf team, was a regular caller; so was a representative of the University of California at Los Angeles. One morning at breakfast Faldo opened a letter from Tom Weiskopf who was beating the drum on behalf of his and Jack Nicklaus's former university, Ohio State. Wake Forest were also chasing Faldo, but later dropped out.

After taking advice from Keith McKenzie, then the secretary of the Royal and Ancient, and Ian Erskine, secretary of the English Golf Union, the Faldos selected Houston, reasoning that the weather would be warmer in the south. At the beginning of 1976, Faldo, Sandy Lyle and Martin Poxon, a promising amateur from the Midlands, all flew off together to sit the Houston entrance exams. Faldo was hardly an experienced traveller. The longest he had been away from home prior to this was the month he had spent on an outward bound course in 1972.

The entrance exams lasted for fifteen hours. Lyle failed his and returned to Shropshire, but Faldo and Poxon passed and, as a result, were awarded scholarships of about £450 to cover lodging and tuition fees. Faldo also received free food, although as the University all but closed down on Sundays his father had to meet this expense as well, in addition to paying for Nick's air ticket and providing him with pocket money.

Poxon loved it in Texas. 'The golf facilities were outstanding,' he says. 'We could use almost any club in Houston and they all had so much space. There were always large practice areas, greens to pitch to and lovely putting greens.'

But Faldo was ill at ease right from the start. To his surprise he was expected to work for three hours each morning, studying subjects such as Physical Education and Public Speaking. He didn't like that and quite quickly began to skip classes. Nor did he like the competitive structure of American collegiate golf. Used to practising for hours and then playing at least one round a day at home, he found his routine was turned upside down. He could scarcely ever practise and almost every afternoon he was expected to play competitive rounds, the results of which would determine who was in the team that week-end.

Nevertheless he put up creditable performances and was selected for three of the University's five matches. He also won a freshmen's tournament with a two-round of 140. 'But I was losing so much time,' he says. 'I was dependent on the other guys in the dorm for a lift to the course each afternoon and at the week-ends they always wanted to lie in after going to discos the night before, whereas I wanted to get going. They were so lazy! I was practising once a week, at the most, and I was falling behind. I knew it.' At the beginning of March Faldo asked his father to get the entry forms for the coming amateur season in Britain and then booked himself a flight home. He landed back at Heathrow on March 14th, less than ten weeks after leaving England.

Poxon, incidentally, did not stay much longer than Faldo. He found the competition fierce and only once represented the University. Towards the end of his first semester he was told that the authorities had reduced the number of scholarships and were reluctantly forced to end his. Without any money with which to continue, Poxon returned home.

There are two schools of thought about this episode in Faldo's life. One is that he showed no character in giving up so soon, complaining of – among other things – having to share a room and to study. I subscribed to this view.

Micklem holds the other viewpoint. He says that Faldo was far-sighted and brave in realising his golf wasn't improving and thus deciding to quit. As should be obvious by now, Faldo was determined to succeed in golf and he was secure in the knowledge that he always had the support of his parents. He never had any of the normal adolescent worries; or if he did, then he wasn't affected by them. He was a loner from the day he was born. When he began competing in amateur tournaments he always preferred to have his own room rather than to share with a fellow competitor, because this way he felt he would sleep better. It was this single-minded determination that made him quit Houston so quickly. As Micklem points out, what was thought to have been a lack of character at first subsequently turned out to have been the demonstration of a lot of character. Faldo proved that champions must learn to cope with failure.

Faldo arrived back in England in March 1976 and soon after won the King George V Trophy at Craigmillar Park, Edinburgh. But his turning professional was imminent. 'I felt as though everybody was expecting me to win in Scotland' he says. 'And as that would have made it much harder if not impossible to be as successful as I'd been the previous year I decided to turn pro.' He did so on April 14th and in August became a member of Mark McCormack's stable. Some time earlier McCormack had been tipped off about this hot-shot amateur who was bound to turn pro and as soon as he could McCormack hurried to Sunningdale to play a round with Faldo. He was impressed. Faldo was everything Micklem had said he was. McCormack was even more impressed when Faldo took British golf by storm towards the end of the following season – thereby proving he had been right to leave Houston and that his critics, myself included, had been wrong.

In August 1977 he captured his first title, a 36-hole strokeplay event at Gleneagles, sponsored by Skol Lager, and, by way of celebration, he treated his parents to dinner at the hotel. A few weeks later Faldo was selected for the Ryder Cup, the youngest player ever, and was unbeaten in foursomes, four-balls and singles. Hardly had that finished than he won the Laurent Perrier Trophy, an eight-man invitational event in Belgium, from a field that included the Americans Hale Irwin and Billy Casper and the young Spaniard Seve Ballesteros, the dashing hero of the previous year's Open.

Early in 1978 there came another example of the high regard in which Micklem held his young friend. Faldo was preparing for the Open at St Andrews when he received through the post four foolscap sheets of instructions from Micklem as to how best to play the Old Course. Micklem had learned everything he knew about the most famous golf course in the world from playing in the 1946 Open with Leonard Crawley, the distinguished amateur and subsequently golf correspondent of the **Daily Telegraph**. He wanted to pass on his knowledge, and to whom better than Faldo, whose rousing play he had admired so much in the recently-staged Colgate PGA Championship at Birkdale. Faldo had indeed been impressive, romping away from a high-class field to win his first four-round strokeplay event by seven strokes.

'Gerald pointed out everything about St Andrews,' says Faldo. 'Every bunker, hump and hollow, the effects of different winds and even where the pins might be for each round. He explained where to drive the ball in order to have the best approach to each green. I was most impressed to think that he had written all this while sitting at his desk in Sunningdale. He is a genius.'

Playing professional golf is lonely work, being out there in front of hundreds – sometimes thousands – of pairs of eyes, not to mention the television cameras. Apart from family and his childhood friends, the person who can offer the pro the most comfort is the man with whom he spends the most time, his caddie. In Faldo's case this is Dave McNeilly, a tousle-haired Ulsterman. Faldo hired McNeilly in May 1982, just after returning to Europe for the summer. On the eve of the Martini International at Lindrick, Yorkshire the two of them spoke to each other on the telephone. Questioning McNeilly closely about different aspects of caddying, Faldo asked him about yardages. 'Do you have a wheel?' he said, meaning a wheel for measuring distances. McNeilly, who was somewhat nervous at the prospect of being engaged by Faldo, spoke up clearly and firmly: 'No,' he said, 'I prefer to use public transport.'

That was the first of many misunderstandings and differences the two of them had at the start. By his own admission McNeilly was inexperienced and of no help to his new employer. A few weeks spent with golfers attempting to pre-qualify on the competitive American circuit was hardly the sort of training necessary to prepare him for employment by a golfer who had finished second in the European money list the previous year.

McNeilly was lackadaisical and because his concentration was bad he was prone to give the wrong yardages on some shots. An explosion, typical of many in those days, occurred during a round at the Sun Alliance PGA Championship at Hillside, a tournament eventually won by Tony Jacklin after a thrilling play-off with Bernhard Langer. McNeilly gave Faldo a yardage on one hole. 'You have 105 to the flag,' he said, as he stood with Faldo looking towards the green. 'Looks further to me,' Faldo replied. 'I'll check it again,' said McNeilly. He paced it off once more. 'It's 118 to the flag,' he said when he returned. Faldo exploded. 'For Chrissake, make your mind up!' he shouted at his caddie. 'I'd better go and do it for myself.'

'I can look at a yardage and eyeball it pretty exactly,' says Faldo. 'If my caddie says 156 I might say it doesn't look as far as that. It only looks 150. So you have to check it again and there's a doubt as to who's right. In the end you split the difference. Yet even that is not good enough when three yards can make the difference between staying on the green and going over the back and having no shot.'

Hot-tempered as Faldo is, others are more so. Ballesteros kicks his bag in anger and constantly mutters at his caddie when things go wrong. Worse still in his treatment of caddies was the American Mac O'Grady, who made seventeen attempts to qualify for the US tour before being successful. O'Grady, whose real name is Phil McGleno, is a genuine eccentric. He can play golf almost as well left-handed as he can right-handed and he is apt to say things like: 'Right now I'm going through a catatonic, neurosomatic disorder. I'm in total emotional upheaval.' For a time he competed on the European circuit and any caddie who worked for him for more than a month was accorded a long-service medal by the other caddies. Few caddies lasted more than two weeks.

Nothing is more distracting to a player than for him to feel unable to trust his caddie completely. Both caddie and player want a relationship in which, as John Moorhouse, one of

Faldo's earlier caddies, puts it, 'The golfer believes you, the caddie, are right. If it's between a six and a seven iron and you say seven you want him to play it without worrying that it is the wrong club.' Faldo's rule is clear: 'If I take a club out and you've got a slight doubt about it then keep your mouth shut,' he told McNeilly, 'but if you're ninety or 100 per cent confident I've got the wrong club then shout.'

By the time of the 1982 Open, Faldo and McNeilly had ironed out most of their differences. 'Those first few months were pretty rough for us,' recalls McNeilly casting his mind back to that glorious spring and early summer. 'It was going through those tough patches at the start, which went on for two or three months, that made me realise how intolerant Nick is of mistakes. If I made a mistake on the course he wouldn't hide his displeasure. He wouldn't make a subtle attack on the next tee. The outburst would be made in public, there and then. It would be very embarrassing for me. He was right, though. It was my mistake and because he was such a hard taskmaster I learned quicker than I would have done had I been with somebody who was more tolerant.

'The most difficult time to caddie is when things are rough,' McNeilly continues. 'Even though he's coming down on you it's very important to make sure your job is not affected by that. It can be hard, learning what to say at that time. You can't possibly hold grudges. He will say things on the spur of the moment and if I held that against him then I couldn't work for him. We've had our differences on the golf course but, to give Nick his due, afterwards it's all over and done with.'

The Faldo-McNeilly partnership prepared meticulously for the Open at Troon. While McNeilly checked and checked again all his yardages, Faldo played two practice rounds with Tom Watson, as well as three on his own, and, in addition, hit at least 200 balls a day. It wasn't unusual for them to start warming up just after nine in the morning and not finish until 6.30 or later that evening. Such hard work was rewarded when Faldo finished joint fourth after a fine 69 – one of the day's lowest scores – in the last round. That was the turning point in their relationship.

'I had looked around to see if there was another caddie,' Faldo says, 'but the only one I wanted was Dave Musgrove and he was working for Sandy Lyle, so I decided to carry on with Dave. My results were good, he was somebody to talk to and he had a good sense of humour.' When Faldo, putting beautifully, won the Haig Whisky Tournament Player Championship at Hollinwell, which got him into the Suntory World Matchplay Championship at Wentworth, McNeilly had every right to feel he had completed his apprenticeship.

Different in personality, they share the same sense of humour. Faldo, introduced to the Tony Hancock records by his mother, had, in turn, passed on his enthusiasm to McNeilly. In exchange McNeilly often quotes from Rowan Atkinson's **Live in Belfast** cassette. When Faldo gets too tense, as he often does, McNeilly uses humour to break the tension. He has been known to turn on his boss in mock anger and snarl, **pace** Atkinson, 'I wouldn't trust you to sit the right way round on the lavatory.'

Faldo's temperament is such that he often needs a lift. The first demonstration of McNeilly's ability to raise Faldo's spirits came in the 1982 Carrolls Irish Open after Faldo had struggled in a high wind and scored a 78. He was desolate and sitting by himself in the changing room when McNeilly found him. It so happened that the caddie had headphones on and was listening to the Peter Cook and Dudley Moore creations, Derek and Clive. Removing the headphones, McNeilly gave them to Faldo, saying, 'Have a listen to this Nick. This is much more important than what went on today.'

Moments later a posse of journalists arrived to quiz Faldo about his 78 and were astonished to see him helpless with laughter. It was five minutes before they could get any sense out of him. A phrase from Derek and Clive has entered the

Faldo-McNeilly lexicon. Whenever Faldo hits a particularly good shot McNeilly will call out: 'A picture in the paddock and beautifully turned out'.

The two of them are working on a routine they hope to try out next time a microphone comes to eavesdrop as they discuss which club to use. Faldo starts it off: 'How far have I got, Dave?' 'You have 176.24 yards to the pin,' replies McNeilly. 'The wind direction is north-north-east at five miles an hour and don't forget that as this is the 14th hole there is a personal fatigue factor of 14 or 76.40%.' Back to Faldo, staring hard at the green: 'The grass is growing at a rate of 0.003 millimetres per second so we must take into account the drag resistance factor of the club on the grass.' Consulting his watch, he continues: 'It is now 11.31 in the morning. The sun still isn't fully up so there will be five per cent moisture on the green, which will slow down the ball by three miles per hour between the second and third bounce.' And so it goes on.

Spectators at a tournament may see Faldo and McNeilly walking down a fairway laughing and joking to one another. It's possible that they are imagining the degree of difficulty of Faldo's next shot but more likely that they are in the midst of some whimsical conversation begun by McNeilly to raise his boss's spirits. 'He's probably describing his favourite tennis shot, which is the half-volleyed overhead backhand smash drop shot,' says Faldo.

At times like these Faldo is at his least demanding, requiring McNeilly to do little more than carry the clubs, keep the irons clean and help with yardages. Unlike many of his contemporaries Faldo always reads his own putts. It becomes much more difficult for a caddie when his player's game goes to pieces. Then the caddie has to know what to say and when, or if, to say it. Some golfers, and Mark James is one, don't want any consolation at all from their caddies. But Faldo needs communication constantly, as a plant needs water. From the moment he begins his warm-up prior to his round to the time when the clubs are replaced in the locker at night, Faldo wants to feel it's a shared experience, the two of them against the rest. Accordingly, he encourages McNeilly to comment on his swing. 'He should know a bit by now,' says Faldo. 'He has watched thousands of my swings over the years and he always wants to know what my swing thought was for each shot. He is good at spotting the little errors that creep in. He says things like: "You picked that one up a bit," or: "Your head's moving a bit too much." '

In making these analyses it helps that McNeilly was once a promising golfer himself, playing to a handicap of three when he was in his mid-teens. He knows those moments when golf is the easiest game in the world, when not even a downhill chip from a bare lie can hold any fears. He also knows how wretched the game can be and perhaps this is why he is so good at offering comfort to his boss. Recalls Faldo: 'After the last round at Augusta in 1984 he said to me, "Don't worry. You played great this week. You were so determined on the first tee, much more than last year when I thought you looked rather nervous. I just don't think the ball went your way, that's all." '

In return for carrying a golf bag, wearing a player's watch during a round, cleaning the clubs, calculating yardages and fetching balls on the practice ground, some caddies receive a weekly wage topped up with bonuses when their player earns any prize money. McNeilly is paid a percentage of Faldo's gross winnings. The vicarious pleasure derived from being so closely associated with someone so good at golf is another form of payment. 'When I took up caddying it wasn't my intention to make it my career and money was not the objective,' says McNeilly, who had formerly worked in a tobacco factory in Carrickfergus. 'I just liked to be involved. Now I am involved I suppose I'm beginning to view myself as a full-time caddie.'

He summed up his contentment at the recent turn his life

has taken and, at the same time, gave Faldo a compliment with a typically wry remark. The two were caught in a thunderstorm during a tournament in Yorkshire. As rain whipped into their faces and thunder rolled around overhead they knew they had to find a more solid refuge than Faldo's large golf umbrella particularly as forks of lightning were flashing over the course as well. They were about to make a dash for it when McNeilly turned to Faldo, who was wiping rain from his face, and said, 'You know Nick, I still think you have the best job in the world.'

CHAPTER 3

Annus Mirabilis

Even in moments of wild optimism Nick Faldo could hardly have dreamed of having a year such as he had in 1983. He entered sixteen tournaments in Europe and won five of them, three of his victories coming successively. No player had done that in modern times when the standard is so much higher and the competition fiercer than it used to be. In all he amassed £140,000 in prize money, another record, and a sum he could scarcely have comprehended seven years earlier when as a tall, slim youth with a fresh face and a willowy swing he had turned professional. He led the world with his stroke average for the season, ahead of his hero Jack Nicklaus; his European rival Seve Ballesteros; and his friend Tom Watson, whom he had beaten in the singles of his first Ryder Cup. All this and more in one year. It was indeed an **annus mirabilis**!

Until then there had been no doubt that Faldo was a very good golfer. As early as February 1981 an American pro named Bruce Fleisher played with Faldo in a tournament in San Diego and then asked, 'Nick's got a beautiful swing. Is he cleaning up in Europe?' Faldo wasn't cleaning up but he was winning tournaments that mattered: three PGA champion- ships in four years, as well as victories in three other tournaments. He had competed brilliantly in the Ryder Cup since his debut in 1977. And year in and year out he finished among the leading money-winners in Europe. But Faldo was so promising it didn't seem good enough that he had won only an average of one tournament each year since turning pro. A harsh assessment of his performances up to the end of 1982 might have been a **beta** plus.

Faldo's slow start to 1983 gave no indication that he was about to burst out so spectacularly in the year of his twenty-sixth birthday and his seventh full season as a pro. In fact, it appeared rather the opposite, as he began with a series of poor results in tournaments in the US. His best finish from the first six tournaments he entered was sixth place at Greensboro. In the Masters he started well only to fall away; the next week he missed the cut.

He and Melanie decided to have a break and they headed for Dallas for some rest and recuperation. But even that was a disappointment initially. They went sightseeing to a local lake, having been assured it was breathtaking, only to find it looked like any British reservoir. Southfork, which had seemed so glamorous when they watched Dallas on television at home in England, was a let down, tawdry and situated opposite a shanty town of motor homes. 'It took only ten minutes to walk around and cost four bucks,' says Faldo. 'It was a rip-off.' To cap it all, they didn't do any house-hunting, which had been one of their main reasons for going to Dallas. And yet the key moment of Faldo's entire year, the ten-minute conversation that made everything that followed so successful, occurred in Texas after Faldo had played a four-ball with his friend Mark O'Meara against Charles Coody and River McBee, the pro at the Las Colinas club.

Faldo had dragged some shots left during this friendly round and afterwards O'Meara said he thought he had detected why Faldo had a tendency to do this. 'You're too shut, Nick,' he said, as they sipped drinks in the Texas sunshine. 'I noticed that because I have a tendency to do the same thing.' Faldo listened as eagerly to O'Meara as he would to anyone he thought was offering sound advice. He is not one of those players whose ears are closed to all but his own teacher. 'What do you want me to do?' he asked, picking up a club and addressing an imaginary ball.

'Try opening the club more on the takeaway,' O'Meara suggested, bending down and holding Faldo's wrists and then rotating them slowly as he began his takeaway. 'Try rolling your wrists over the moment they start the backswing.' Later, on the practice ground Faldo tried it. The first few shots flew everywhere. It felt odd but he persevered, oblivious to everything but his search for an improved golf swing. For the next five days he did little but hit balls at Las Colinas and when he had finished he didn't turn to O'Meara and say 'Eureka I've got it', but he **was** left with a feeling that he had learned a lot about his swing.

The new swing had its first test that same week. To Faldo's pleasure he finished joint 21st in the Byron Nelson Classic, three under par. He had little time to dwell on it because he had to dash to the airport to catch a flight to London and thence Paris. After receiving a 'phone call late on Saturday night from IMG in London on behalf of the organisers he had agreed to replace Greg Norman in the following week's Paco Rabanne French Open. Norman had withdrawn after undergoing an operation on his leg.

As the Faldos flew home I was busy on a project I had thought of in February after a lunch at the Royal Overseas League, a handsome Edwardian building in a small courtyard off St James's Street, London, to which I had been invited by the English Golf Union. This lunch was an annual occasion, the main purpose of which was for the EGU to introduce their President-elect to the golf writers, over some decent beef and good red wine. It was civilised and low key – a model of the way in which to deal with journalists.

The conversation moved from subject to subject as fast as

the hands of the clock until, as the port appeared, it settled upon the new handicapping system that had just been introduced in England. According to Ian Erskine, the secretary of the EGU, the adoption of this system had caused outbreaks of something akin to butchery by handicapping committees up and down the country. Erskine took his glasses from a jacket pocket and slipped them on to his nose. Reading from some notes he had made, he reported in his **basso profundo** voice that in the first six weeks of its operation nearly sixty golfers who had formerly had a handicap of scratch had now been downgraded to a handicap of one or more. 'The new system has had the effect of a force twelve gale,' said John Cheatle, then President-elect of the EGU. Apparently, only six men were left in England with plus handicaps.

Riding back to the office in a taxi, I wondered what would be revealed by a similar scrutiny of the pros. It was taken as read that they could play well below par, but how would they fare over a season containing twenty-seven tournaments on as many different courses? I bought myself some sharp pencils, a ruler, an eraser and several sheets of the largest graph paper I could find. I wrote the players' names down the left of the paper and the name of each tournament along the top, allowing for six rounds to be filled in, two qualifying, and then four in the tournament itself. Then I had to make some decisions. I chose to place the pros in category one handicap, the same as the lowest amateurs. I was thus able to raise their handicap by decimal point one if they played one or more strokes above the standard scratch score and to lower it by point one for every stroke they were below the SSS. I adjusted their handicaps at the end of each round, not at the end of each tournament.

After the season's first three tournaments a pattern began to emerge on my chart: the best players were improving their handicaps; the worst players were struggling to remain at scratch. Bernhard Langer, who had competed in all three events, was down to plus 1.1 after winning the Italian Open. Tunisian champion Mark James and Seve Ballesteros were the same, each having played two tournaments. Sandy Lyle, victorious in the rain at Madrid, was down to plus 0.3. Had I scrutinised Faldo similarly, as I later did, I would have found that his rounds of 71, 69, 72, 69 in Texas were sufficient to give him also a handicap of plus 0.3.

Arriving in France Faldo vowed he was going to win more than one tournament that season. 'It's time to see what you're made of, Faldo,' he said to himself as he nibbled fruit in his hotel room in Paris. 'This is the season to do something.' He decided not to allow himself to be flustered by the poorly-mown fairways, the bumpy greens and bad weather he knew he would experience in Europe. 'I'll just get my head down and get on with it.'

He began steadily over the par 72 course at Racing Club de France, La Boulie. His new swing held up nicely and with scores of 69 and 67 he found himself level with Seve Ballesteros. Carl Mason was in the lead. He'd had fine rounds of 68 and 66. Faldo's third round was disappointing, being seven strokes worse than David J. Russell's, but he played more steadily in the last round and when he reached the 18th tee he was only two shots behind Jose-Maria Canizares. The Spaniard had chipped into the hole on the 17th to gain the lead. Now came the first indication of how Faldo's time in the States had toughened him.

He had always been able to rise to the occasion – his outstanding Ryder Cup record proved that – and he produced a cracking drive and a skilful and long two iron second shot to reach the green on this par five. His ball came to rest 15 feet from the hole. An eagle, he reasoned, would give him a chance of a play-off. His putt went in, Canizares missed his birdie and they were into a play-off. David J. Russell was knocked out at the first extra hole. Canizares and Faldo halved the second and on the third extra hole Canizares hit into some bushes handing the tournament to his opponent. Faldo was delighted at his first victory in a four-round Continental Open, one in which he was so little known he was listed in the programme as Mick Faldo. Later that night his car screeched to a halt outside the house in Ayot St Lawrence of a friend, Danny Desmond, and he held the trophy over his head. 'Look at this mate,' he seemed to be saying. 'All my own work.'

In the Martini International at Wilmslow, Cheshire, the next week the weather was as wet as it had been in Paris. It was hard to believe it was the middle of May. Faldo's first practice shot blew so far off course that it smashed the windscreen of Hugh Baiocchi's car. Fortified by soup made by the landlady of the digs where his caddie Dave McNeilly was staying, Faldo raced through the field on the last day. With two 66's he caught Canizares again and once again he defeated the Spaniard on the third extra hole of a play-off.

It was as well for McNeilly that his boss won. McNeilly committed the unforgivable sin of turning up late for the last two rounds on the Sunday. As Faldo fumed, McNeilly raced to the course, arriving only minutes before Faldo had to tee off. Faldo, his temper not improved by a heavy cold, decided that if he didn't win then he would fire McNeilly. 'I've got to have a reliable caddie' he thought to himself. Thus did victory bring Faldo a handsome cheque and, at the same time, spare what was to become one of the tour's most successful partnerships from breaking up.

Faldo had always worked hard on his golf. Now he seemed to be working harder than ever and again he was often the last to leave the practice ground at the end of the day. Perhaps this was why he was able to summon up that little bit extra when he wanted it, as, for example, at the start of the last round at Wilmslow when he began with six birdies in seven holes. Somewhere, too, he had learned how to win play-offs. Don't make mistakes, was his motto. Keep the ball in play.

The least obvious improvement in his game was his ability to score steadily when he was not quite at his best. Apart from moments of brilliance, Faldo ground out the figures, knowing that if he did that long enough he would wear down his opponents. That is precisely what happened. Wherever they looked Faldo was quietly getting on with the job, holing a long putt for a birdie, a tricky five-footer for a par. For a while speculation in the dressing room was not predominantly concerning Seve, and the most frequent question asked was: 'Where's Faldo?'

This was brought home clearly a week later in the Car Care Plan International tournament at Sand Moor, Leeds. Again it was wet and windy but Faldo played patiently and let others complain about the bumpy greens. Tony Jacklin referred to them as Yorkshire puddings. Faldo deliberately practised on the putting green even though it was far from smooth, reasoning that if he could get a rhythm there then he could get one out on the course. It worked. He holed many crucial five-foot putts which were the key to his success, and won the title by one stroke. It was his third victory in succession and in as many weeks and it equalled Peter Alliss's three-in-a-row in the Opens of Italy, Spain and Portugal.

Because of his success in the foul weather. Faldo was christened 'The Rain King'. During lulls in play in those early wet tournaments McNeilly liked to tease his boss. 'Ladies and gentlemen welcome to Wilmslow,' he would say in his version of a commentator's reverential tone while holding the cover of a wood to his mouth as if it was a microphone. 'You join us just in time to see Nick Faldo getting out his waterproofs. Nick Faldo is going to don his waterproofs. My goodness ladies and gentlemen he is even putting the trousers on one leg at a time. He's ascending the two steps to his throne. Ladies and gentlemen, The Rain King is in his element, he is on his throne.'

In terms of the weather the three weeks had been far from

memorable but in all other aspects Faldo could hardly have had a better time. In twenty-one days he had won £31,954, almost half as much as in the whole of the previous season. It worked out at just under forty pounds for each stroke. Faldo was heartened, too, at the way his new swing had held up in the far from clement conditions. 'My swing change gave me something to concentrate on for each shot,' he says. 'I knew if I did it, then I would hit a good shot and if I didn't, then every shot would be a bad one. So it was simple. As I walked up to my ball I asked myself a question: "Do you want to hit a good shot? You do? Then I suggest you make sure you fan the club open on the takeaway."'

His scores brought his handicap tumbling down. Eleven of his 12 rounds were under 70 and he was 31 under par for those 222 holes. No wonder he had the lowest handicap on my chart. As he prepared for his fourth tournament in Europe his handicap was plus 2.7. Lyle was the next best pro, with plus 2.2; Ballesteros was plus 1.7 and Ken Brown plus 1.5. At the other end of my chart, by contrast, were the strugglers. Jeremy Bennett, for example, was finding it very hard to fulfil the promise recognised in him by Henry Cotton in 1981 when he received Cotton's rookie of the year award. His handicap had risen after each of the six tournaments he had competed in. So too had Gary Logan's. Bennett was now playing to 1.2, Logan to 0.9.

The next week our paths split, as in midweek I went to the Walker Cup at Royal Liverpool while Faldo pressed on to practise at Royal St George's, Sandwich, for the Sun Alliance PGA in hopeful though not realistic pursuit of some of the records set by the American Byron Nelson in 1945.

That was Nelson's year to end all years, a time when he entered thirty tournaments and won eleven of them in a row. Try as Faldo might, it was certain he couldn't match another of Nelson's achievements – that of winning money in 111 successive events. Faldo, though beginning to tire, was still thinking aggressively. Before the second round of the PGA he told me at breakfast, 'I say to myself now, "This run doesn't have to end. If someone is going to beat me then I'm going to make sure they've worked for their victory. Let them come and get it from me."'

After winning the 1980 Sun Alliance PGA at Sandwich and then spending hours in preparation for the following year's Open at the same course, Faldo knew the splendid links of Royal St George's as well as anyone. For two rounds he was in with a realistic chance. At halfway he lay one stroke behind the leaders, Ballesteros and the Irishman Des Smyth. His opening 72 was only his second of more than 70 since he had returned from the US at the beginning of the month. But a tired 74, his worst for four weeks, sent him tumbling down the field and eventually Ballesteros was acclaimed the winner.

Faldo was far from finished. Perhaps inspired by a fine performance in the Open at Birkdale, where he led momentarily on a thrilling last afternoon, he took the Lawrence Batley International at Bingley St Ives. He had wanted a rest, the events at Birkdale having left him exhausted, but he was prevailed upon to play. A 64 in the third round without birdieing any of the par fives thrust him right to the front. Then he as good as closed the doors on his competitors with another of those devastating bursts – nine under in 15 holes – for a last round of 62 and victory by four strokes. His 64 and 62 equalled the 36-hole record in a tournament in Europe that Tom Haliburton had set in the Spalding tournament at Worthing in 1952.

Ronan Rafferty is well qualified to pass judgement on Faldo, having played with him in the last round. 'He gave me the impression that he shot 62's every day of the week,' says Rafferty, a note of surprise evident in his voice. 'When he got six or seven under par he still didn't stop or even ease back. Somebody else might have started using a three wood off the tee to protect their lead but Nick fired his driver down the fairway, hit great irons to the green and putted like God. He went out and won the tournament. He didn't wait for it to come to him. The guy's got bottle.'

He had now won more than £75,000 in this his **annus mirabilis** and his handicap on my chart was down to plus 4.2. When you consider the quality of some of the courses he had competed on – the Sven Tumba Country Club in Sweden, Royal St George's in the wind and rain, Birkdale in the Open – this was outstanding scoring. He was £31,000 ahead of his nearest challenger for the title of Europe's leading golfer, a prize that would guarantee him invitations to the US Masters, the World Series, the Suntory World Matchplay Championship and sundry other events. He was prepared to go anywhere and do almost anything to win the Harry Vardon Trophy, which is awarded to the player who tops the European money list.

With his new swing working so well and everything else falling into place, Faldo had good reason to be thankful he had remained loyal to his caddie Dave McNeilly who had been so inexperienced when they began working together at the start of the 1982 season. Their relationship had now become strong enough to withstand an incident that occurred on the 18th green in the third round of the Open at Birkdale. Faldo, cheered to the skies by raucous supporters, needed to hole a 10-foot putt for a par. It would have put him into joint second place with Craig Stadler, one stroke behind Tom Watson.

As Faldo squinted at the putt from one end, McNeilly checked the line from the other. 'It's a little bit left to right, I reckon,' Faldo said when they compared notes. 'If you think that you're absolutely wrong,' said McNeilly surprisingly firmly. 'I saw Arnold Palmer have the identical putt this morning and it definitely broke from right to left.' A worried look appeared on Faldo's face. It wasn't often that he and McNeilly disagreed like this. Nevertheless, he took his caddie's advice and was about to putt when his concentration was broken by a noisy spectator shouting: 'Come on Nicky baby!' Faldo backed off, regained his composure and then struck the putt. It broke to the right and missed and Faldo gave McNeilly an icy look. When they met the next morning Faldo had with him a newspaper which mentioned this incident beneath the headline 'Big Mouth puts off Faldo'. Handing over the paper, Faldo remarked drily, 'Right headline, wrong person.'

In September, after the Panasonic European Open at Sunningdale, Ballesteros had closed on Faldo in the race. Faldo declined to be best man at his brother-in-law's wedding the following Saturday and instead flew to Switzerland to participate in the Ebel Open-European Swiss Masters. It was not a decision he could make very easily for he knew he would offend his wife's family. He was swayed by his father-in-law who told Melanie that Nick should go to Switzerland, an opinion later endorsed by BBC TV commentator David Coleman when they met by chance in a hotel in Cornwall. 'You're a professional sportsman,' Coleman told Faldo. 'It's your job to play. Go and do it.'

By the time of the tournament in Switzerland Faldo had won £94,650 in eighteen weeks compiled from four victories, two second places and three thirds in thirteen tournaments. The confrontation in Crans sur Sierre was between him and Seve Ballesteros, two men with burning ambition. Faldo was desperate to win the money list; Ballesteros, if he had to concede that, at least wanted to win more money worldwide than any other golfer. Including lucrative victories in the US Masters and the Manufacturers Hanover Westchester Classic, Ballesteros had already amassed £250,000 and his victory in the Million Dollar Challenge in South Africa, and its attendant enormous prize money, was yet to come.

At first it looked as though neither could possibly catch Sandy Lyle who had rounds of 64 and 63 and was 11 shots clear of Faldo with only 22 holes remaining. But then came one of those swings of fortune that make golf so fascinating. Faldo finished his third round with three birdies and an eagle and was only five behind Lyle. On the last day, a cold and blustery one, he got three more shots back on the outward half of the first nine. By the 15th Faldo had levelled with Lyle, having gained 11 strokes in 19 holes.

Lyle's 45-foot birdie putt on the last green, which would have given him victory, horseshoed around the hole. Faldo had a 10-foot putt to birdie the last and force a play-off and he holed it. They both parred the first extra hole and then on the second Lyle missed from 14 inches, his ball catching the right lip and staying out. Faldo's fifth victory had come about no less stunningly than had Lyle's victory by 2 and 1 over Faldo in the previous year's World Matchplay. At lunch Faldo had been six up.

Five victories between the first week of May and the second week in September helped Faldo to set all sorts of records in 1983: he became the first player since Bernard Hunt 20 years earlier to win five 72-hole tournaments in one season in Europe; he set a new low stroke average of 69.03 from 64 competitive rounds; and he won £119,416.

What pleased him as much as anything was discovering that he led the world in the stroke averages published in his manager Mark McCormack's **World of Professional Golf Annual**. Faldo played 8,347 strokes in 119 rounds and took an average for each round of 70.15. By comparison Seve Ballesteros came fourth in the table with 70.53 and Tom Watson was ninth with 70.81, even though both had the advantage of playing fewer rounds – 102 (Ballesteros) 74 (Watson). No wonder Faldo has framed this table of players and hung it in pride of place in his bedroom.

At the moment of his victory in Crans, Faldo's handicap reached a lower point than that of any other professional. After his rounds of 70, 64, 68 and 66 it stood at plus 4.3. Since his handicap at the start of 1975, his golden year as an amateur, had been three (it was plus one by the end of the season) Faldo was playing at least seven shots better in 1983. He mulled over this significant statistic for a while and then said, 'It's an even greater difference, actually, because very few amateurs can play to their handicaps. They can move around, select the competitions they compete in. They can protect themselves. Pros can't. Our courses are set up tougher and we have to learn to conquer them. I suppose the moral is that if you can't win as an amateur then you can't win as a pro. Somebody may disprove me but it's going to take a helluva long time.'

It wasn't quite over yet because in October in the Ryder Cup Faldo preserved his unbeaten record in singles and then came joint second in the Walt Disney World Golf Classic in Orlando, Florida. In December Faldo finished joint second behind Ballesteros in the Million Dollar Challenge. Wherever he looked he saw only men handing him money or gifts. He earned $110,000 in Sun City and, every bit as important, as he is a car enthusiast, an Audi Quattro for finishing nearest to the flag on one hole. The final accolade came just before Christmas. Faldo was elected Player of the Year in the annual poll conducted by the Association of Golf Writers.

In success Faldo was gracious, admittedly not a difficult task as everything had gone his way. But he had had to learn how to win just as he had how to lose. As he reflected on the flurry of victories he cast his mind back even earlier to the Berkshire Trophy, his first major amateur win in 1975. 'It felt absolutely fantastic,' he recalls. 'So fantastic I can still remember the feelings of excitement nearly ten years later. I rushed to the 'phone to tell my parents but they were out. I drove home in Dad's Opel Kadett with the windows down, the cup on the back seat, singing and shouting.'

'The true feelings of winning,' Faldo continued, 'can last for ages and ages. It starts at the prize-giving when you sense that people are looking at you. They're not looking at the guys who have come fourth tied, they're looking at the winner. They want to see the winner. But it can go on for longer than that. After that there's the time when people are saying "There's Faldo, he won last week." And then after that the feelings of success can remain inside you for ages. There have been pressures on you to win, and so finding that you have met them is rewarding. You've pushed yourself and you've found that you're not scared of winning.'

He has learned how much the British prize a sense of decorum in their victors. 'You have to get away from the club with your feet on the ground. You're not really meant to leave the car park in your Jensen with the wheels spinning, the radio blaring and a blonde by your side. That's what I remember one amateur doing. For the mature guys, winning is merely their **task** for the week and if they win they have done their job well. They've met their target. It is as simple as that. You mustn't kiss the mayor's wife, leap around the place and generally make an exhibition of yourself,' Faldo continued. 'You mustn't brag about it. You can state a fact, saying "Yes, I played well this week," but I know that everybody wants to think that you know you've had the golfing gods on your side.'

While Faldo's phenomenal success was being recorded on the sports pages, other sections of certain papers were chronicling his marital matters. He and Melanie had had a troubled relationship for some time and throughout 1983 it became steadily worse. The time Faldo spent in the US in 1981, 1982 and 1983 may have been the making of him as a golfer; it was also the wheel on which his fragile marriage finally shattered.

CHAPTER 4

The Wheel of Misfortune

All had not been well between Nick and Melanie for a couple of years, but they had remained together as though they were determined to give their marriage every chance in the face of flurries of rumours. George Faldo recalls being told by a colleague at work as early as 1980 that his son's marriage was on the rocks; similar rumours had been circulating on the golf circuit.

His parents now believe that Nick and Melanie rushed into marriage, showing all the lack of caution that twenty-one-year olds are noted for. George Faldo suggests that if they hadn't insisted on marrying before the Ryder Cup in the autumn, then they might not have married at all. Joyce Faldo agrees with her husband. 'It was a very fiery courtship,' she says. But marry they did, in June, 1979, after Nick had romantically proposed to Melanie over a candlelit dinner on Valentine's Day.

They made an attractive-looking couple. Faldo was tall, handsome and successful. He had won nearly £40,000 in prize money the previous year. Whether he really was or not, he gave the impression of being sophisticated as he moved from one hotel to another, one country to the next, this continent to that. Melanie, who was a few months older, brought to the marriage a dowry of intelligence and a loyalty that was to reveal itself time and again in the coming years.

She found Nick more mature than many of her student contemporaries at the University of Warwick. 'His single-mindedness and determination appealed to me,' she says now. 'He seemed a very strong, relaxed character. He knew what he was doing. I felt he would take care of me.' Her parents and brother had taken to her new husband as well. Of the boyfriends Melanie brought home, Nick was the first her father approved of. 'I like Nick,' he told Melanie one day. 'He's a real man.'

In those early days Melanie had few plans other than to be with her new husband. She assumed her future would be divided between the time spent accompanying Nick to tournaments abroad and time at her new home, Tudor Cottage. She and Nick shared this with his parents for six months, until George and Joyce Faldo moved out and went back to Welwyn Garden City. In addition to running the house Melanie made some of Nick's hotel reservations and travel arrangements, as well as attending to correspondence on a small portable typewriter set up in the dining room.

Melanie knew very little about golf. She found it a frustrating game to learn, just as she found it frustrating when, while following Nick around the course, she would overhear derogatory comments about him. 'Look at that Faldo, he's always in the rough,' or 'What a terrible shot! I could have done better.' Only once did she lose her temper and then she rounded on a man and snapped at him, 'If you think you can do better, then I can arrange a challenge match with Nick Faldo any time you like.'

Her loyalty to her husband could never be criticised. She once wrote a stinking letter to the host of a radio phone-in programme who dared to refer to Nick as a 'cry baby'. Another time, feeling he needed to be spurred on, she told him of a newspaper article she had read about the tennis players John Lloyd and Chris Evert.

In this article Evert was quoted as saying that her husband had more natural talent than she but that she possessed the greater will to win. 'You have an awful lot of natural ability Nick, and the determination that will make you a winner eventually but sometimes you don't apply it as well as you should,' said Melanie. 'Be determined!' Inspired by this advice, Faldo went on to end a bleak spell by winning the PGA at Sandwich.

She came to understand his temperament and mannerisms so well that if she didn't know from a scoreboard how he was doing, she could tell just by seeing him walk a few steps. In the second round of the 1980 Suntory World Matchplay Championship Faldo had been four up on Greg Norman at lunch and apparently storming home. But his body language was so expressive going down the 18th in the afternoon that Melanie, who had not been watching up to then, immediately knew that something was wrong. She noticed that his head was down and he was dragging his club and, sensing the worst, she crept into the clubhouse while her husband and Norman began the extra holes.

Norman won, as Melanie knew he would, defeating Faldo at the 38th. Faldo was despondent at his collapse and he drove home in almost complete silence. In the narrow drive of the house they had been staying in during the tournament, he unpacked the boot of the car. When he got hold of his bag he raised it over his head and hurled it, clubs and all, into the garden. Although he went to Paris for the Lancome the next week, he didn't really regain his appetite for golf for a month.

Defeats in matchplay cut Faldo to the quick. 'You have all the nervous feelings of winning a strokeplay tournament just in beating one guy,' he says. 'To be up and then see it all go is a horrible feeling.' Faldo should know that feeling if anybody should, for in addition to that defeat by Norman there was the famous occasion at Wentworth when he was six up on Sandy Lyle with 17 holes remaining – and still lost. 'The fact is that everybody has seen it,' Faldo once explained. 'TV have shown it going wrong and 5,000 people watching at Wentworth have seen it going wrong. It's not like some guy having a rotten day at the office when only he and his secretary know about it. You get the feeling that everybody is looking at you and you wonder to yourself, "What the hell do I look like?" You can't hide. Nobody can hide emotions. You can't come up the last fairway thinking, "It's great to have been six up and now to have lost," and to wave at everybody.'

In January, 1981, Faldo flew to the States to try for the card that would entitle him to play on the lucrative and competitive US circuit without having to pre-qualify for each tournament. It was the first of three long trips he and Melanie were to make across the Atlantic at the start of each of the next three years and, if they did but know it, it was the beginning of the end of their marriage.

Faldo took to life and golf in America like a duck to water, in a way that Sandy Lyle, who arrived at the same time, did not. Within days of his arrival he had adopted the peacock colours American golfers favour and he relished the perquisites of unlimited golf balls, gloves and clothes that came his way. After watching him in California I wrote in the **Sunday Times**: 'There is something purposeful about the tall, straight-backed Englishman. He goes about his business with a brisk precision that suggests he is a no-nonsense man on and off the course. Arriving in San Diego at lunchtime last Tuesday, he raced to the course and, by hurrying, squeezed in 18 holes on one of the two courses he would have to play in the tournament and nine holes on the other. Melanie, meanwhile, had unpacked their luggage, done their washing and brought their book-keeping up to date. Faldo returned as dusk was gathering, ate a typically hearty meal and was sound asleep by 10.30.'

Success came quickly, more quickly than either he or Melanie could have dreamed of. He compiled a stroke average of 71.5 in his first nine rounds. A sensational 62 in the Hawaiian Open, a course record, was marked by a headline in the local paper: 'Faldo's 62 is a jolly good show.' Faldo was playing better each time he stepped onto a course and no one was surprised when, by the end of his fifth tournament, he had already surpassed the $9,000 he needed to earn his players' card. In those five events his results had improved from joint 77th to seventh.

Melanie, however, soon began to get rather bored with it all. Each morning she would take out a small travelling iron and press the shirt Nick had chosen the night before. More often than not it was a shirt she had washed, for he hated most hotel laundry services.

Walking behind the ropes at tournaments she became friendly with some of the wives. Many of the others she felt were shallow. She got to know Jackie Traub, Lisa Powers and Alicia O'Meara, an engaging lady who carried a little dog around in her handbag as she supported her husband Mark. But often Melanie would go for weeks on end without seeing these friends because their husbands either hadn't made the cut or had chosen to take the week off.

On days when she didn't go to the golf course Melanie would stay by the hotel pool and write her journal or play tennis. Not having a car she found it difficult to do any sightseeing. She read voraciously and, because she could never bear to throw books away, every couple of months would wrap those she had finished with in a parcel and send them home to England. An irony of which she was only too aware was that she was in the country whose art and literature she had studied at University and yet she felt she had neither the time nor the opportunity to go out and explore it.

In short, life was not particularly fulfilling. 'When I realised that I had only one choice and that was to be with Nick as much as possible and to a large extent take care of his affairs, then I did that for the first three or four years and enjoyed it. But somehow there was always a little voice inside me that said, "Something's wrong". I'd look around at the girls who were having babies and whose husbands were on the golf tour and were enjoying themselves and it wasn't that that bothered me. I'd look at girl friends I'd been with at school and University and it was seeing them beginning to make headway in their careers that upset me. I was envious of their outlet for themselves. Being a golf wife is a terribly secondary existence. You're always orbiting around an enormous star. You're never shining on your own. You exist only as a satellite.'

By 1982 Faldo was established in the US and as they criss-crossed the country from tournament to tournament Melanie found it helpful to look forward to the day when they would have a home in the US to which she could return from time to time. Though they looked at houses in Dallas, near their friends the O'Mearas, nothing came of it and soon Melanie was pleading with Nick to go out occasionally in the evening to the theatre, cinema, even roller skating, just to break the monotony. 'I was screaming out for some kind of life, whereas he would play golf for twelve hours a day, come back to the room, have a shower, go out to dinner and then go to bed.' They talked half-heartedly about starting a family though they both realised this was some time off. First, they needed a base in the US.

The disenchantment Melanie had first begun to feel in the US soon spread to her life in Europe as well. 'It was a gradual realisation that if Nick couldn't give me more of himself or employ his time with me in different ways, then I questioned what role there was for me as his wife. I never said, "I don't want to be your wife any more," or "I don't want to support you." I would just say to him, "Look, can't you help me? I want to be a good wife but I feel that in trying to be so I am giving everything I've got to you and I'm not getting anything back."' She even tried returning to work, but all that happened then was that she fell between two stools. She didn't get on very well with her job and nor did she look after her husband.

Throughout 1983 the rumours about them grew louder as Faldo was seen to be on his own more and more. He was becoming increasingly lonely and he found precious little comfort at home. 'We didn't have much of a home life. We never sat down and had a relax. It was all so hectic. Come and see this, do that, see this. I'd come home, throw the clubs down and fiddle around. I just wasn't happy at home. Golf was my escape. I went to the course, enjoyed it and won. If I had to be at home then I would fiddle with my clubs or go and see Barry Willett (the clubmaker at St George's Hill, Weybridge). But even that could cause an argument. Melanie wanted me to come home and stay at home. I would go to one end of the house and put on my music full blast. I had my snooker table there and I played on that a lot. She would be up the other end of the house, in the kitchen probably. We were in the house but we were apart, we didn't get in each other's way. It was a means of keeping the peace.

'I thought that America was going to be a new horizon for me and with my career at the stage it was I had to go and play there. Melanie hated America and hated touring. That's when it all came to a head. That was a major factor in our separation. I couldn't be expected to make a serious campaign over there with her not being fully supportive. I wanted her to be with me. I wanted someone to talk to, to help me, to share my experiences.'

There weren't loud rows with bitter accusations being shouted back and forth. Doors were not slammed and nor were there days or even hours of pursed lips. Melanie did once or twice storm out of the house and go to her mother's for an afternoon. From time to time as they each sought something the other could not give they talked first of separation and then divorce. Yet Melanie was constantly reminded of a saying she had heard on the radio late one night. She was so impressed that even without turning on the bedside light she reached for the pad she always kept nearby and scribbled it down: 'The secret of success is the ability to survive failure.'

But there was no surviving this failure and the more Melanie surveyed the ruins the more she found herself casting envious glances at a couple who also lived in Ayot St Lawrence, the pretty Hertfordshire village that had also been the home of George Bernard Shaw for nearly fifty years. 'They were both lab technicians and they used to go to work on a motor bike in the summer and in a small car in the winter. They only had a tiny house and probably not much money but to me they had something we never ever had. Although we had all those shared golf experiences, we never had anything that was completely our own.'

One of the last experiences that the two of them did share was the searing incident in the match against Graham Marsh in the World Matchplay at Wentworth in October, 1983. (Why does everything happen to Faldo at Wentworth?) At the 16th hole in the afternoon he and Marsh were all square when Faldo's second shot scuttled through the green. Moments later it reappeared four or five feet in the air and it came to rest back on the green. It had obviously been thrown by a patriotic spectator.

Faldo was unsighted, being 150 yards away at the time, so was Marsh and so was Melanie, who was behind the ropes 50 yards from the green. Unfortunately the referee was unsighted as well. He took the word of a green-side official and, after failing to find evidence to the contrary, ruled that as the ball had not stopped moving Faldo was entitled to play it as it lay, this enormous piece of good fortune coming under the heading of 'rub of the green'.

Marsh was a perfect gentleman and accepted the ruling, but a good many spectators were appalled on his behalf, for it seemed to offend that most British characteristic, the sense of fair play. What they had seen was clearly unfair and they didn't mind saying so. 'I am British and proud of it, but as far as I'm concerned I hope Faldo three putts,' one spectator said to me. To make matters worse Marsh then missed the three-foot putt (and some spectators cheered) that would have given him a four and Faldo won the hole with a four. He won the next hole as well and so took the match by 2 and 1.

Faldo was upset and embarrassed by what happened. Subsequently he was furious at the attacks made on him by journalists, who felt he either could have conceded Marsh's second putt or been more gracious in victory. 'What I did was right,' he maintains. 'I came up to the green innocent. Why should I have given him a three-foot putt when I hadn't seen what had happened. You wouldn't walk up to somebody and say, "Here is ten pounds." I worried about it for a long time afterwards and then I realised I was right. What I did was right. So I told myself to stop worrying.'

By December the marriage was at an end. Faldo spent most of the evening of December 30th, 1983, lying on the sofa at Tudor Cottage watching television while Melanie was on the telephone in the kitchen making arrangements for New Year's Eve. Towards the end of the evening Faldo announced he was contemplating leaving home. He was persuaded to stay and the next day went out for a drink with his friend Danny Desmond who tried to talk him round. Faldo did indeed remain at Tudor Cottage until it was time for him to fly to the US. The day before he left Melanie packed his suitcases, turned up six pairs of trousers and drove to Northampton to collect some new golf shoes for him. She intended to remain in England, half thinking that she might join her husband near the time of the Masters in April.

Soon after Faldo landed in America, Gill Bennett flew out to join him. In a 'phone call to Melanie early in February Faldo admitted that Gill was with him. Melanie immediately began divorce proceedings. On February 9th the news broke. 'Star golfer Nick in Love Tangle' was the **Sun**'s huge headline on the front page. Reporters laid siege both to Melanie, who was all but kept a prisoner in Tudor Cottage for three days, and to the room in the Hyatt Regency Hotel on Waikiki Beach, Hawaii, that Faldo was sharing with Gill.

For a while Faldo was clearly distracted from his golf by the pressures. At the beginning of February he went close to winning the Bing Crosby Pro-Am in Monterey. A week later, after news of the separation had broken, he missed the cut in Hawaii.

He and Gill were being hounded by journalists. Faldo successfully put a woman reporter telephoning from London off the scent when he pretended to be a butler answering the 'phone in 'Mr Faldo's residence.' But one night in Hawaii a reporter and photographer from the **Daily Star** came upon them at dinner and requested an interview. Nick and Gill declined, left the restaurant separately and were amused when they noticed the photographer was so intent on taking pictures that he backed into a lamppost. Later, these same journalists tried to woo them with a bottle of champagne, which they drank and again refused an interview.

They flew to Australia for Faldo to compete in the Masters, only to find the pressure was as great down there. After being discovered in a restaurant by journalists the two of them made a crafty getaway through the kitchens and an underground car park while friendly waiters created a diversion. 'It's not the parting with Melanie that affects me,' Faldo said to one reporter at the time. 'It's the constant 'phone calls to my manager to find out what is going on in England. Whatever is going on I know I have to put it all behind me and get on with playing golf.'

After his success in the Heritage Faldo's golf began to falter as the year wore on and he found this most depressing. He was supported and buoyed by the constant presence of Gill at his side, but his golf, the most important thing in his life, was increasingly unsatisfactory. 'When you're playing good golf it doesn't matter what is going through your mind because you can cope with anything,' he says. 'On the course I'm good at blocking things out. I don't think of anyone or anything that isn't to do with golf. People think I'm rude because I don't answer them but actually I often don't hear them.'

He couldn't help noticing that now that his marriage had broken down, other things didn't go well either. For example, it took much longer than he and Gill had anticipated for their new house to be ready, and so for most of the year they lived in hotels, or rented houses, or stayed with friends or with Nick's parents. Faldo wanted to be able to relax, to play his records, but there never seemed to be an opportunity. And all the time there were the details of the divorce settlement to be considered.

The fault with his golf was not new and although he had thought that with the help of his friend Mark O'Meara he had remedied it, he still had a tendency to swing too steeply. This was hardly surprising in a man six feet three inches tall. On the backswing he failed to open the clubface sufficiently and as it was still slightly hooded at impact, his shots tailed off to the left. To find the cure he could have returned to his first teacher, as Nicklaus always used to visit his at the start of each year. Or he could have taken some time off. Brian Barnes, had he been faced with a similar problem, would have gathered up his fishing equipment and headed for the nearest trout stream. Or he could try and play it through.

He chose this last course, because he remembered how his golf had suffered when he went through a bad patch in 1979. Undoubtedly distracted by his marriage, Faldo played poorly and slumped from third to 21st in the money list. This time he was determined his golf would come first despite the turmoil of his private life. He practised as hard as ever. In the US in June and early July he wouldn't take a rest even when his hands started to swell and he was patently dog-tired. He was like a man driven by demons. And all the time he was almost certainly doing the wrong thing.

Gill was a source of considerable comfort to him through-out, following him for almost every round and always prepared to wait while he did his interviews or practised some more. 'Gill and Melanie are total opposites,' says Faldo. 'She enjoys travel, perhaps because she is the daughter of a pilot. When I say we're going away she says, "Oh good, we haven't been on a plane for a week." She gets on better with the other wives. We both like the same sort of music. We make instant decisions, whereas before we used to have to have a stewards' enquiry before we did anything. Life is much less complicated now.'

Gill was enjoying every minute of it. She was a novice and the more she saw the more she liked. She quickly fell into a routine of spending the early part of each week around their hotel writing letters, shopping, doing any paperwork that was necessary, so that by Thursday, the first round, she was ready to begin tramping around watching Nick. Even to this seemingly mundane task she brought a routine. 'I don't walk around with my head in the clouds,' she says. 'I pay attention. I'm learning all the time. Sometimes I make notes, mark down where Nick's shots have gone. I always carry a card of the course. It helps me to learn. When they start using golf terminology at the dinner table I can understand what they're going on about.' She was even anxious to have golf lessons in order to help her understand Nick better.

At the first possible moment, often as soon as he had driven from the first tee, Faldo would try and spot Gill in the gallery and then keep an eye on her throughout the round. Knowing that he had one loyal supporter, one who wouldn't leave him and walk into the clubhouse without first telling him, Faldo felt relaxed and happy. It gave him a sense of being in a partnership, the joint aim of which was to make sure he played to the best of his ability. 'It's nice when you come in at the end of the day and she knows that you've had a cow of a round. She understands and doesn't expect you to go through it blow by blow. At least somebody is watching you who has the same feelings as you and can appreciate what you are trying to do.'

'I know what my role is in this relationship,' said Gill. 'At this stage of my life I want to help support somebody else who in turn supports me. I'm old fashioned enough to believe I should stay with him. I would only get a job if I could go off and be with him whenever I wanted to. I don't need to go out and prove myself. I've travelled and had lots of jobs. I'm quite happy to sit back now. I don't think my role is secondary. I don't feel inferior. I can't go out and play golf for Nick. That's something he has to do for himself.'

It was, however, against a background of a loss of form in his golf and tension in his private life that Faldo flew to compete in the US PGA. The championship of the US Professional Golfers' Association is the last of golf's four major championships to be held each year, coming after the US Masters, the US Open and the Open. It is also the least important of the four. The 66th US PGA was held in August 1984 at Shoal Creek, a recently-opened luxurious club set among hills ten miles from the Alabama steel town of Birmingham. As strong a field as any had gathered there in pursuit of the $125,000 first prize.

The money was academic for most of them. They each had their own reason for wanting to win the two-foot-high silver trophy. Jack Nicklaus needed victory to prove he was still a force to be reckoned with at the highest level of the game. For Tom Watson it represented his last chance to capture a major title in 1984; he had been edged into second place in both the Masters and the Open. A victory for Greg Norman would be no more than the talented Australian deserved after the brilliant golf he had played in mid-summer. And were Seve

Ballesteros to win, as he dearly hoped, then it would be another one in the eye for the Americans less than thirty days after he had won the Open at St Andrews, his fourth major title.

For his part, Nick Faldo felt that his banner year in Europe in 1983 and his triumph at Harbour Town in the Heritage in April indicated that he was good enough and ready to win a tournament such as this. Besides, he was anxious to erase the memory of bad performances in the Masters and Open.

Faldo began well at Shoal Creek, scoring a 69. In the second round he reached the 18th hole towards the end of a typically humid day that had sapped his stamina and left his shirt so wet he would later wring perspiration out of it. He had every reason to be content with his day's work so far. While his distinguished playing partner Jack Nicklaus was struggling to make the cut after a lacklustre 77 in the first round, Faldo was playing as well as he had the previous day. He was three under par for the round, six under for the tournament, and only three men were ahead of him, Gary Player, Lee Trevino and Lanny Wadkins.

On the 18th tee, with a three wood in his hand, he aimed down the fairway that swooped away and turned slightly to the left until it reached a large green protected by bunkers on three sides and a lake and a bunker on the fourth. Faldo's tee shot flew left, as his bad shots often did, and ended in clinging Bermuda grass rough from where he could only hack out to the fairway with a sand wedge. He then faced a shot of some 160 yards to the flag, which was set near the back and towards the left half of the green.

His seven iron started off line. The more it veered left the more Faldo leaned to the right as if hoping that his body movement would diminish the error. The ball curled and curled until it plopped down in an unplayable lie amidst mud and water on the edge of the lake. He was forced to take a drop and concede a stroke. His delicate chip ghosted past the hole only to gather speed as it rolled down a shoulder in the green. It stopped 25 feet from the flag. He then three-putted, his second putt horse-shoeing around the hole from three feet. He had taken a four over par eight and was never to be in contention again. For the third time in four months he had ruined his chances in a major championship.

That's how it was for Faldo from May until October, 1984. Nothing would go completely to plan. In one tournament after another he would compile four rounds that were individually acceptable yet collectively not good enough. Sometimes he had three good rounds which were then spoilt by one bad one. This happened in the last round at Augusta, causing him to fall from joint third after 54 holes to finish in a tie for 15th. And it happened again at the Open. Rounds of 69 and 68 left him joint second, but then he took a horrible 76 on the third day. On another occasion a good round would be spoiled by one bad hole, as at Shoal Creek. Then, when Faldo thought he saw some light at the end of the tunnel after a 65 in the first round of the European Open at Sunningdale, he walked into trouble again.

On the eleventh hole in the second round he unwittingly broke a rule. He picked his ball from what he thought was a lateral water hazard and moved it two club lengths sideways. In fact it was a water hazard and he should have replaced his ball keeping the point where the ball entered the hazard between him and the flag. He was later reported to tournament officials. There was nothing for it. Faldo had to be disqualified.

Since the end of April, things had gone from bad to worse for Faldo. He retained the Car Care Plan at Leeds but thereafter came third, joint sixth, joint sixth, joint 17th in European tournaments and ended 12th in the European money list, the lowest he had been since 1979. It was his third worst year in Europe in his nine years as a pro. There was a similarly uneven pattern to the way he played in the US. He had made a storming start and after the Heritage had accumulated nearly $150,000. But then he added only a paltry $15,000 from the remaining six tournaments he entered and missed the cut in three of them.

Faldo was in a slump such as every golfer has to endure at some time or another. It happened to the great Jack Nicklaus between 1978 and 1980, to Johnny Miller between 1977 and 1980 and even to Gene Sarazen from early 1924 until the end of 1931. Unused to such hard times, Faldo was frustrated beyond measure. 'At times like this you start asking stupid questions like: "How long is this going to last?" and "Maybe I have lost it for ever." Then you start playing negatively. You stand on the tee and think, "There's no way I can hit this fairway," and when you have a long putt you think, "Uh, uh, three putts here." If you land in a bunker you know you won't get it up and down and when you miss the green you realise you're going to drop a shot. At times like this you're gone, you're out of it. You might as well pick the ball up and walk off the course.'

Hard as he tried to block out distracting thoughts, they crept around his defences more often than he wanted. And once one crack had appeared in the wall of his confidence, then he was powerless to stop other cracks appearing and spreading as well. His golf suffered, the old sore – his relationship with the press – started to fester again; he was practically homeless for months. He had a flaming row with Dave McNeilly, his caddie, during a tournament in the USA. For a time it seemed that everything went wrong.

It all came to a head in the autumn of 1984. While Nick and Gill were in Paris for the Lancome Trophy, Sam Torrance came over and said, 'I see you've been getting a going over again in the press.' It was a reference to that day's leading story in Nigel Dempster's Diary in the **Daily Mail**. Headlined 'Nick nicks knick-knacks' it reported that Faldo had returned to Tudor Cottage and hauled off two vanloads of household items, including a large colour television and a food mixer, rather than, in the words of the article, 'visit a local furniture shop'. 'Rubbish!' said Faldo, by way of explanation. 'It was all arranged with Melanie beforehand. I wish he'd check his facts.'

Faldo had survived six months of a divorce that was threatening to become messy and public. In the eyes of the majority he was the villain because, and he accepted this judgement, he had committed adultery. He knew that golf enthusiasts regarded him as badly behaved. Indeed, there was a letter in the current issue of **Golf World** accusing him of being selfish in the Pro-Am before the Irish Open and insulting his partners by practising his putting while they were holing out. All this Faldo accepted as an occupational hazard of being a celebrity in a business that rewarded him extremely handsomely. But when he had returned to the clubhouse after his round that day and discovered that a thief had stolen his shoes, his temper finally snapped.

'I'm fed up with it all, my game, the press, the divorce, everything,' he said later, having returned to the hotel still wearing his spikes. For an hour he and Gill talked it over until Faldo had cooled down and vowed to start all over again. 'This game is like running an engine,' he said to himself. 'If you try too hard you blow it up. I've had enough of all these things going wrong. My priority is to go out and enjoy my golf again and that will take the pressure off everything else. I'm going to relax in my dealings with the press, give them what they want, worry less about what they write. I'm going to adopt a happy-go-lucky attitude towards my golf for the time being. To hell with it.'

Having thus cheered himself up on this grey, cold night in Paris, Faldo, by now having dinner, raised his wine glass to Gill across the table and silently and hopefully bade farewell to the worst six months he had known for a long time. His new attitude brought quick results for in the next four tournaments he was to win nearly $200,000.

CHAPTER 5

Nick Faldo
(International) Ltd

By the time he started his second quarter century, Nick Faldo had become one of the most successful money-winning golfers ever to emerge from Europe. After nine seasons as a pro he had amassed nearly £500,000 in winnings, his worst year being his first when he had won only £2,112; his best coming in 1983, his **annus mirabilis**, when he won £150,000.

In 1984 his winnings in Europe sank to less than £50,000, though this was more than compensated for by the $160,000 he won in the US where he spent more time than in previous years. Add appearance money of $10,000-$15,000 for each European tournament he entered and the £125,000 he earned by coming second in the Million Dollar Challenge in South Africa at the end of 1984 and one thing becomes clear: Faldo doesn't need to worry about paying the milk bill, even though he has to bear his own expenses in the US and even though International Management Group, which manage him, cream off twenty per cent of his income. In 1984 his worldwide prize money amounted to more than £300,000. Since he turned pro he has won nearly £1.4 million world-wide.

By any stretch of the imagination these are handsome

figures. Faldo's father worked for thirty years and earned less than his son won in four days at the Million Dollar Challenge. I calculated Faldo's hourly rate of pay in South Africa to be a staggering £1,736, based on eight hours work for each of the four days. To get a sense of perspective I thought of my friend Jonah Barrington, who had been the best known squash player in the world, amateur and professional, in his day. The man who had won no more than a measly few hundred pounds on taking the **de facto** world championship in the mid nineteen sixties had an income approaching £80,000 a year by the nineteen eighties.

Perhaps, though, this is an unfair comparison, squash being a sport that isn't shown on television and does not attract large crowds of spectators. A more realistic yardstick might be Steve Davis, the brilliant snooker player, who earned £500,000 in prize money in four years or, for that matter, a top marathon runner who could receive £40,000 for one race. Golf, like snooker, is a high-income business and in Europe at least Faldo is at the very top of it.

Anyway prize money is only half of his income. From designing Hot-Blade putters and using, wearing or endorsing Pringle shirts and sweaters, Hertz cars, Pioneer stereo equipment, MacGregor golf clubs, Sunderland rainwear, Bena Travel, ICI Fibres and Glynwed products, and most recently, Daks shirts, sweaters and trousers in Japan, Faldo earns at least as much again.

He is fortunate to have a very good physique – broad shoulders, slim waist, long legs and no more fat on him than a marathon runner. Pringle, ready to expand their production of golf clothing, soon realised the potential of the tall Englishman and signed him, initially for three years, when he was still a rising star. 'Nick is a nice young Brit who presents the sort of image we want for our products,' says Graham Hayward, Pringle's marketing director. 'He is a smart person himself and he makes a good model for our clothes. He has a good figure.

Obviously it wouldn't be any good to use a player with a paunch.'

Both parties to this contract have benefited from the quality of British television which can present golf in colours every bit as bright as a Hockney painting. At Pringle's headquarters in Hawick, Scotland, a phenomenon has been noticed. The morning after a golf tournament featuring Faldo has been transmitted on television, the factory is inundated with orders from people asking where they can buy 'sweaters like the one Faldo was wearing yesterday'.

Not surprisingly, Pringle are one of the largest of Faldo's contracts. At the other end of the scale are Glynwed, the Midlands-based industrial giant making bathroom and kitchen fittings. The man who did this deal was Sir Leslie Fletcher, an engaging golf enthusiast who is chairman of Glynwed International. We met in his office in the City. At one point the telephone rang on his desk and he ignored it. 'Sod it,' he said, 'I'd rather talk about golf anyway.'

Fletcher had been tipped off about a promising young English pro by Sir William Barlow of the Post Office. Standing together on the side of the fairway during the 1977 Open at Turnberry, Sir William said to Sir Leslie, 'This chap Faldo needs some help. Come on Fletcher, you can help him. I can't. I have enough on my plate at the moment. But you're in engineering. You can do something for him.'

A few days later Nick Faldo went with his father to see Sir Leslie in London and a deal was worked out. In return for a few thousand pounds a year Faldo would have a Glynwed sticker on the bottom of his bag and Glynwed International (or their subsidiaries in other parts of the world if Faldo was playing there, Defy in South Africa, for example) after his name in tournaments. In similar fashion Bernhard Langer represents Ready Mixed Concrete Group, West Germany; Seve Ballesteros the Spanish resort of La Manga.

It was Glynwed's first venture into this kind of sponsorship, though they had rented a tent in which to entertain customers and clients at Turnberry and had had boxes at several football grounds in the Midlands. The money involved was so small that the chairman could authorise it without any reference to his fellow directors.

'They came to my office and as I sat looking across at Nick I couldn't help noticing his large hands,' remembers Sir Leslie. 'I thought to myself, "The clubs must look like pencils in them. With hands like that he **must** be able to play golf."' Thus was started Faldo's longest contract and since then Sir Leslie has become not only a friend of Faldo's but also one of his most-travelled followers, having turned up on courses as far apart as Augusta, Georgia, and Sun City, Bophuthatswana, South Africa.

'Our relationship is commercial, but it's not really commercial,' says Fletcher. 'I suspect he costs us less than we have to spend on putting our half-yearly figures in the paper. He has carried the Glynwed flag with great distinction. He has done nothing for our sales and, I suspect, nothing for our share price, but there is something to be said for people commenting when you mention the name Glynwed, "Ah, yes, you're the people who are involved with Faldo." He is like a racehorse for us. What he costs us goes a long way round the Group as internally people ask: "How is Nick doing?" That is every bit as important as outside advertising.'

Another company whose products Faldo endorses is Pioneer, the Japanese firm who makes hi fi and car entertainment equipment. 'Any form of sponsorship is icing on the cake,' says Bill Budge of Pioneer, who is assistant to the managing director. 'What you are trying to do is to get people to know your brand name. This type of sponsorship goes to a wider audience than conventional advertising. Golf is popular in terms of the number of people who participate and watch it so if you can get your name in front of those people you are indirectly doing a good advertising activity. You're not advertising your product on the page, you're projecting it a stage further from your advertising campaign. It's brand awareness, I suppose. If a lot of your distributors and the people who service your operation, like the ad agencies and banks, also participate in that sport it's good because it becomes a sort of business social occasion when you can get together with people readily, with nothing very formal about it. Rather than seeing your banker across a desk you might get him out to play golf with you. From time to time he might even be able to play with Faldo, which is good for him and therefore good for us, too.'

Pioneer also sponsor the London Philharmonic Orchestra, the Glyndebourne Festival and Ipswich Town Football Club, all activities that straddle the conventional boundaries of advertising and marketing. 'If I had just a set amount of money then I would advertise my product,' says Budge. 'But this is marketing and when you're marketing you have to have a product, a price, some form of distribution to get your product known.

'Then you have to tell people where to go and buy it. You can either advertise it or make sure shopkeepers have it on display in their windows. Then you have to persuade people about the merits of Pioneer. Most of this is by word of mouth, though advertising does help. Now, if you bring sponsorship in on top of all this so that when someone goes to a football match they see a Pioneer sign or a team wearing the Pioneer logo on their shirts, then this is reinforcing all the things you are doing. I think that the more you mix things up sensibly the more attractive you make your company product.'

For most of the companies with which he is associated, Faldo – in return for their largesse to him – does one or more company days a year. These are relaxed occasions, when the hosts wine and dine some of their most favoured business associates and Faldo plays a few holes of golf with them, advising on their grips and their backswings, explaining how to read putts and what to do when faced with a downhill chip from a bare lie. He usually gives a clinic after lunch, playing shots off his knees, between his legs, with one arm. He has a special trick shot with a club he calls his leather mashie (it's his shoe actually) and he demonstrates how to get out of the rough with it. It's at times like this that Faldo comes to life and confounds his public image of an uncommunicative, self-interested pro. This was what struck Robin Ellis-Bextor, film director for BBC Television's **That's Life** programme, after he had watched Faldo first on **A Question of Sport** and later in a filmed sequence for the popular Esther Rantzen programme. This lighter side of Faldo's character also comes through in the BBC's **Pro-Celebrity Challenge** series.

'We heard about this four-year-old boy, Richard Wheatley, who wanted to play golf with either Seve Ballesteros or Nick Faldo,' says Ellis-Bextor. 'We decided to use Faldo because we considered he had the highest profile of British golfers. He was wonderful with the little chap, very professional. A lot of sportsmen don't know what to do, they turn up late, they don't seem committed. He wasn't like that at all.' Faldo won himself a host of new followers by arriving for the filming with a tiny rain jacket and miniature putter specially made for his young opponent. By way of a token appreciation for Faldo's performance, and no doubt grateful that he had done it for nothing, the BBC gave him a rare thank-you: a bottle of champagne.

There are certain products that Faldo refuses to endorse. A non-smoker himself and, incidentally, a regular runner capable of covering a mile in well under six minutes, he won't have anything to do with tobacco advertising. On the advice of his manager John Simpson, he is very chary about promoting drink. On the other hand, Simpson was keen for Faldo's name to be used in a radio and poster campaign on behalf of the Egg Marketing Board in the autumn of 1984 – 'Nick Faldo's tea'. Simpson reasoned that taking Faldo's name into a

The Association of Golf Writers awarded their own trophy to Nick Faldo for 1983.

ast act of Nick Faldo's reign as holder of
Heritage title came on the eve of the 1985
t. The defending champion, Faldo
ed the traditional tartan jacket given to
winner, and smacked a ball into the
d off Hilton Head Island and, as near
ltaneously as possible a cannon was
. Moments later Faldo posed peacefully
he cannon with the famous Harbour
n lighthouse in the background and a
band prepared to entertain the
ators who had assembled in the warm
h Carolina sunshine.

The five trophies: the French, the Martini International, the Car Care Plan, the Lawrence Batley and the Ebel Swiss Open that Faldo won in 1983. *(Phil Sheldon)*

Tony Jacklin (non-playing captain) congratulates Faldo after his brilliant performance in the 1983 Ryder Cup which so nearly brought a surprise result for the European team. *(Phil Sheldon)*

Melanie Faldo.

Sometimes a golfer's life can be glamorous. *(Alpha)*

and, sometimes not. *(Dave Cannon)*

Winning The Open remains Faldo's major objective – and over the past eight years he has the best record by a British golfer. In 1983 at the Royal Birkdale he led after 58 holes but eventually finished joint eighth, five strokes behind Tom Watson. *(Phil Sheldon)*

The 18th tee at St Andrew's, scene of The Open in 1984: Faldo illustrates the perfect swing. *(Dave Cannon)*

Nick Faldo tees off at the short 11[
hole with the Old Course and the tov[
of St Andrew's in the backgrour[
(Dave Cannon)

In the 1984 Masters in Augusta, Fal[
was well placed after three rounds ([
69 and 70) but slipped to joint fifteer[
with a final round of 76.

(a) The Sarazen Bridge beside the g[
at the long 15th hole. *(Dave Cannon)*[

(b) & (c) bunkered *(Dave Cannon)*
(d) an unusual back swing. *(Phil Sheldon)*

The agony (a) failing with a birdie at the 18th.
The Open, Royal Birkdale, 1983. *(Dave Cannon)*

(b) The Suntory Matchplay, Wentworth, 19
(Mike Powell)

(c) The Open, St Andrew's, 1984. *(Phil Sheldon)*

and the ecstasy (d) The Car Care Plan, 19
(Phil Sheldon)

Faldo has proved a popular figure on BBC2's Pro-Celebrity Golf, and Pro-Am tournaments give the golfers a chance to relax. Faldo shares a joke with Jimmy Tarbuck. *(Dave Cannon)*

And just occasionally there's a prize worth winning too! Faldo with his Audi Quattro that he won for a 'nearest to the hole' competition at the 1983 Sun City Classic. Nick has a penchant for fast cars and enjoys watching Formula 1 motor-racing. *(Dave Cannon)*

Faldo with Peter Oosterhuis in the 1981 Ryder Cup at Walton Heath. They lost to Tom Watson and Jack Nicklaus, 4 & 3. *(Dave Cannon)*

Faldo and Sandy Lyle. Lyle's form in Europe in 1984 will keep Faldo on his toes in 1985. *(Phil Sheldon)*

thor, John Hopkins, posing at
e Open, St Andrew's, 1984.
hil Sheldon)

John Simpson at the 1983
Masters. Simpson, a vice-
president with IMG, is Faldo's
manager. (Lawrence N. Levy)

Nick Faldo and Gill Bennett.
(Alpha)

Nick Faldo with his caddie Dave
McNeilly. *(Phil Sheldon)*

Sometimes it's a pleasant walk in the countryside, sometimes it's not:
(a) signing autographs. *(Dave Cannon)*

(b) landscaped putting. *(Dave Cannon)*

(c) using a reversed club. *(Mike Powell)*

(d) spot the ball. *(Phil Sheldon)*

W.B.—19795

THE COLGATE P.G.A. CHAMPIONSHIP 1979

THE OLD COURSE – ST. ANDREWS
17th, 18th, 19th and 20th May, 1979

Match No. 27   Date 17TH

COMPETITOR   NICK FALDO

Marker's own Score	Hole	Yards	Par	Comp. Score	Hole	Yards	Par	Comp. Score	Marker's own Score
5	1	370	4	3	10	342	4	4	4
4	2	411	4	4	11	172	3	2	3
4	3	371	4	4	12	316	4	3	3
4	4	463	4	3	13	425	4	4	4
5	5	564	5	4	14	567	5	6	5
4	6	416	4	4	15	413	4	4	4
4	7	372	4	4	16	382	4	3	3
3	8	178	3	2	17	461	4	4	5
5	9	356	4	4	18	354	4	3	4
	OUT	3501	36	32	IN	3432	36	33	
					OUT	3501	36	32	
					TOTAL	6933	72	65	

MARKER'S SIGNATURE

COMPETITOR'S SIGNATURE

FOR OFFICE USE ONLY

P/Q	1	2	TOTAL	3	TOTAL	4	TOTAL

(e) a record round at the Colgate PGA Championship, 1979. *(Steve Powell)*

(f) at the short 14th on the West Course at Wentworth. *(Dave Cannon)*

(g) Winning the Car Care for the second year in succession. *(Phil Sheldon)*

broader marketplace than golf would enhance his client's image and was well worth doing even though the £1500 fee was lower than Faldo normally received.

'To pinpoint the areas in which you can market a client you have to know the client well; have to know what he's happy with,' points out Simpson. 'The way the Pioneer deal came about was that I was looking for a company outside golf to sponsor Nick's golf bag. First, I had to find the company and then I had to sell the idea to them. Now there are two things outside golf that Nick Faldo likes doing. One is driving cars and the other is listening to his stereo. There was no car manufacturer for whom it would have made sense for Nick to carry anything on his bag and so I went straight to the stereo people. The third company I spoke to was Pioneer.

'Sponsorship used to be much more of the chairman's whim kind of thing than it is now,' Simpson continued. 'The chairman or managing director thought that because Nick Faldo had a great swing they should sponsor him and take Nick down to the golf club on a Sunday morning and show him off. That is a thing of the past. Now it's much more professional and usually a part of an overall marketing plan. For example, C and A wanted Sebastian Coe because they'd never done any sponsorship before and they wanted this upmarket image. Nick's deal with ICI Fibres is more hinged on: "We're a British company in the US, Nick Faldo is a British golfer in the US. He is one of the most up and coming golfers on the tour and we want you to meet him."

'We all know you can influence businessmen. I know what happens when Nick does a golf day in Greensboro or some customers are invited along to watch him play and have a meal with him. They have their picture taken with him and then he goes and wins a tournament. The picture is on their desk back in the office and their colleagues come in and see it and remark on it. It's good for their egos and they never forget it.

'The best example I've ever had of this way of doing business was when Boeing held a week-end at Gleneagles for some of their favoured customers. At the airport there were private planes flying people in from all over the place. The first night Boeing took orders for three planes and so the cost of the week-end was paid for one hundred times over. It gets people away from the hassle of the office. It's an ideal way if not of making a deal then of achieving better relations that will enable a deal to be made later, of corporate seducing if you like.'

Faldo became a client of Mark McCormack's International Management Group in 1976 and has been managed since 1978 by Simpson, who joined the company that year. Simpson specialises in looking after golfers, though he also manages Sebastian Coe and Captain Mark Phillips. McCormack claims that IMG are unrivalled in sport and marketing and that his firm, which has altogether thirteen offices in eleven different countries, have representatives of forty different sports on their books.

'You have to have the best available professional advice,' says Faldo 'and when it comes down to it you really can't get past McCormack's. I know the empire's enormous and people wonder, "How am I going to be treated?" but they have different departments. IMG also organise golf tournaments. It all helps. People think that McCormack's have got a monopoly on golf and they say that must be wrong. But if you get in there and you're part of it then you can get into these tournaments. Whether that is right or wrong, you're making money which is what you're employing them for. They do your income tax and all that sort of thing. You know that whatever problems you have you're not the first client to have had them. They've done it before. They're doing Bjorn Borg's taxes. Imagine his and Arnold Palmer's tax problems.'

Faldo has a contract with them that in June 1984 was renewed by both sides for five years. This is a similar contract as exists between IMG and Arnold Palmer, Jean-Claude Killy, Bjorn Borg and Michael Parkinson – to name but a few. They have become millionaires, some of them many times over, and now Faldo is well on the way to becoming one as well. He is generally unostentatious and low-key and possesses a strong sense of financial prudence instilled into him by his father. Years ago George bought shares in Cunard and Nick bought some from his father. Nick would appear at breakfast and with a mouth full of Weetabix ask, 'How are my shares doing, Dad?' Another financial lesson: Nick received his pocket money each month because that was how George was paid and it was how he expected Nick to be paid. The pocket money was accompanied by a warning. " 'There it is, son," Dad would say. "You can spend it on what you like but you're not getting any more until next month. That's your lot." '

Faldo has no desire to become a member of Lloyds or an angel to a stage production in London's West End. Such ventures are too risky for a man who says, 'I'm interested in gambles – so long as they're guaranteed.' He has few indulgences, the chief being the Porsche, which is owned by his company, Nick Faldo (International) Ltd. 'When you get to the stage where you can play with a chunk of money and not mind if you lose it, then that's when you gamble. At the moment I'm looking for the best returns. I want it to keep growing.'

Browsing through the papers one day, George Faldo noticed that the price of port was rising fast. 'I think you should buy some,' he told Nick, who bought not only three dozen cases of Warre's 1970 vintage, but also three dozen cases of each of the highly-rated clarets, Chateau Trotanoy '76 and Chateau Brane-Cantenac '75. It is all held for him by Corney and Barrow, the Queen's wine merchants, in cellars in the City. His first thought is that it will make him money when sold at auction in a few years. Secretly, though, he hopes that in ten years time he will be so successful that he can afford to drink it himself. But typically cautiously, demonstrating that not every one who makes a lot of money at an early age is a spendthrift, he says wryly that if all else fails he can always open a restaurant and sell the wines to his customers.

He has a portfolio of coins, mainly Islamic, which are said to be a sound investment. A much bigger investment are the 360 acres he owns on a remote hill in Scotland, forty miles north of Inverness, which he bought in December, 1983. Roads and fences are being built each year and sitka spruce and lodge pole pine trees are being planted. In ten years it is forecast that the increase will have been two and a half times his original investment.

Faldo invests in shares on the London, New York and Tokyo stock exchanges. He bought some of the twenty-eighth issue of National Savings certificates and as many Jaguar and British Telecom shares as he was allowed to. His investments are overseen by Sean Kelly, an accountant in IMG's London office. 'We're obviously trying to make Nick as much money as we can but we have to bear in mind that his income may falter one year,' says Kelly. While he is still earning large sums the emphasis is on capital growth, though these should give him income as well.'

Currently Faldo's biggest single investment by far is the £100,000 house in Windlesham, a few miles down the A30 past Sunningdale, which he and Gill moved into in the autumn of 1984. It is the third property he has owned. He sold the first, a flat, in Broadstairs, Kent, in 1982 and the second, Tudor Cottage, a 15th century, half-timbered building in Ayot St Lawrence, Hertfordshire, after his divorce from Melanie. With the proceeds he financed Melanie's settlement and bought the Windlesham house.

A modern, four bedroom town house in a terrace of eight, it was built in 1978 on the site of what was once a rather grand residence standing in fifteen acres. It is reached from the road by a half-mile-long drive that passes through clumps of rhododendrons and stands of cedar, chestnut and fir trees. Grey squirrels are to be seen scampering up and down the tree trunks and foxes and badgers live in the undergrowth.

From his front door Faldo could aim straight at the westerly end of Sunningdale's famous Old Course, two miles away. A large lawn, the size of three football pitches and serving all eight houses, runs from the end of his fifty-foot-long, thirty-foot-wide garden to the edge of the woods. On the day I visited, if you had been looking for some sign that one of the houses was owned by a highly successful young sportsman you would only have had to look at the cars parked outside Faldo's house: a Porsche 911 turbo, flame red in colour, and a white Audi Quattro, which was then up for sale. Both had personalised number plates.

It is easy to see the attractions of the area. The M25 is ten minutes away; Heathrow Airport no more than twenty minutes' drive. At a pinch Faldo could be in the West End in fifty minutes or on the M1 and heading north in the same time. Little wonder that its position, not to mention the practice facilities of both Sunningdale and Wentworth, has made this corner of Berkshire as much a magnet for professional golfers as Gloucestershire has become for members of the Royal Family. There are enough colleagues of Faldo's within ten minutes' drive – Sandy Lyle, Bernard Gallacher, Ronan Rafferty and Michael King being just four – for them to team up and issue a challenge to allcomers.

Faldo has a long way to go even to approach another McCormack client, the legendary Palmer, whose disparate companies are said to have earned him an astonishing £230 million in 1984. However, if Faldo were to have four inspired rounds and win a major championship his life and income would change dramatically, as did Tony Jacklin's after he won the Open and the US Open within eleven months of each other. Already a rich man, Jacklin subsequently became a millionaire and sought to protect his status by becoming a tax exile in Jersey.

For the present Faldo trails him in terms of national recognition and has not yet acquired the promotional appeal of Sebastian Coe either. 'Seb is a household name,' explains Simpson. 'All the mums know Seb. He's big in the High Street. Nick hasn't broken through to that extent yet. When he does, that's when the whole thing will break open.'

CHAPTER 6

Inner Golf

At the end of his first round in the Million Dollar Challenge in South Africa in December 1984, Nick Faldo was heading back to his hotel room when he was unceremoniously stopped by a middle-aged lady with a kind face. He wasn't in the best of moods after taking a six on the last hole, which had cost him the lead. Now he was one stroke behind Seve Ballesteros. What this lady had to say was arresting. 'I will make you win this tournament,' she said to Faldo. 'You don't need to practise. You just talk to me for fifteen minutes.' Sensing that Faldo was not quite sure of her, she thrust some newspaper cuttings about herself into his hand. 'Come on,' she said. 'What have you got to lose?'

That first day they talked for a half hour in the clubhouse. 'She gave me a formula for everything, including my private life,' says Faldo. 'She told me how to have a relationship. She gave me a list of do's and don'ts. She told me all about my relationship with Melanie. She knew everything. She certainly had the gift of the gab. At the end of our first conversation I thought to myself, "What **do** I have to lose? I'll give it a go."'

Réné Kurensky, though Faldo didn't seem to know it, had helped a number of golfers with mental problems. Nick Price, Johnny Miller and Tony Jacklin among them. Jacklin in particular was warm in his praise for her in the book **Tony**

Jacklin: The Price of Success by Liz Khan. He said she had helped him particularly with his putting problems in the mid sixties and again in 1977. Kurensky was a scientologist who had played poor golf until she put her mind to it and, using some of the techniques she was about to try and pass on to Faldo, reduced her handicap and won several minor competitions at her club.

When they sat down to talk for the first time Kurensky came quickly to the point.

'What are your intentions this week?' she asked Faldo.

'If I play well, I might get a chance to win,' Faldo replied.

'Wonderful, great,' said Kurensky, her voice heavy with sarcasm.

'That's no damn good. If you want to win how do you intend to win?' She had a habit of emphasising certain words in the course of her normal conversation and this brought home to Faldo how sceptical she was.

'I've got to hit some good shots,' Faldo said. 'If I play well . . .' The rest of his sentence was drowned by a snort from Kurensky.

'If you play well,' she said, emphasising the word **if**.

'If you play well. What do you mean *if* you play well? You're going to go out and hole every shot.'

Faldo looked at her in amazement and then burst out laughing.

'Come on Réné, I can't do that.'

'Yes you can,' she said, completely seriously. 'What's stopping you from holing them? You've got to have proper intentions, Nick. If your intention is to hit it to ten feet then you'll hit it to ten feet. If your intention is to hole it then you'll hole it. From now on I want you to visualise every shot. I want you to pick a target and say, "I'm going to hit my drive there, to that point in the fairway." Then I want you to select your target on the green and aim at that. Rate your shots on a one to ten basis.'

Faldo knew of this technique from some work he had done a few years earlier with Charles Sherno, a man who specialises in performance improvement. At one tournament in Wales the technique had worked brilliantly – for one round. After the second round Faldo had gone straight to the practice ground to hit some wedge shots. Knowing he had only a limited time, he was keen to make sure he practised well. He told himself he wanted a ten from every wedge shot. For half an hour he caught every ball precisely on the right spot on the clubface and they had landed so close to one another he could have covered them all with a small blanket. He surprised himself by how accurately he was hitting the ball. The next day, still excited by his performance the previous night, he had shot a 66. That had been his only good round of the tournament. No matter how hard he tried thereafter he wasn't always able to sustain the visualisation technique for an entire round.

Now, in South Africa, sitting across a table from Réné Kurensky, he remembered the advantages of visualisation – but he quickly realised a disadvantage of it.

'Hang on a minute, Réné,' he said. 'What happens if I've got a one iron across water and the pin is cut into the left of the green, the side nearest the water. I may be intending to hole that shot but I'm human and my nature is to make sure I don't knock it into the water. What happens then?'

'That's all right,' Kurensky replied. 'If your intention is to hit it to ten feet right of the flag then that's fine. That is your thought. If you're happy with that, okay. Just make sure though that you don't settle for aiming ten feet right or twenty feet left when you should be aiming at the hole. I admit there are times when you have to use your experience and say, "A rating of four on this shot is enough. I'll settle for that."'

That made sense to Faldo. He had been in a situation on the 18th in his first round when he should have pulled in his horns a little. He had hit his second shot to the right of the green, leaving himself a tricky pitch to the flag, which was on a sloping part of the green not far from the edge nearest Faldo. He went for the shot, aiming to land it on a small portion of the green, in the hope that his ball would then run softly up to the flag. He was too bold. His chip just caught the edge of the Kikuyu grass and was snared.

'You should have just got it out onto the green and accepted a five,' said Kurensky. 'It wasn't the shot that was wrong. It was your intention that was wrong that time. It's important to know the difference. The first thing you do when you are assessing which club to play is to gather all the information that is available. You have to be aware of the environment. You're a professional, you're conscious of the wind. If you hit a shot and it doesn't go where you wanted you don't say, "The wind got up and blew it off course." You knew the wind was there and was gusting. But you didn't recognise it, and because of that your shot was blown off course. It wasn't the shot that was wrong. It was the assessment that was wrong.'

As she said that a thought crossed Faldo's mind. 'Perhaps my whole year was nothing to do with my golf swing,' he thought. 'Perhaps I played badly because I had no intention, or my intentions were wrong. Perhaps it was that there was too much going on.'

They went to the putting green together.

'Putting is the most important part of the game,' Kurensky told Faldo, as if he didn't know already. Faldo hit some putts.

'Right, now remember what I said about environment,' said Kurensky. 'You have to find out everything about the putt. You have to read the grain, get the line right. How fast does it look? Then when you're 100 per cent confident of everything, then you stand up and hole it. You must be absolutely ready. No room for doubts. If your mind wanders for a milli-second then you'll miss it and you'll have to admit that it wandered.'

Faldo hit the first putt, a 12-footer. The ball just shaved the hole and ended one foot past.

'Why did you miss that?' Kurensky asked.

'I don't know. My thoughts were good,' Faldo replied. 'I did all the correct preparation.' Kurensky shook her head.

'There was something wrong Nick,' she said.

'Okay, you're right. I wasn't concentrating 100 per cent. Let me try another one.'

Faldo took another putt and holed it, then another, then another. A crowd gathered and he began a dialogue with them. 'What will you give me if I hole this?' he asked. 'Two rands?' He sank it. 'Who'll give me three rands for this one?' He holed that one too. He looked at Kurensky. She was enjoying watching him learn. He sank four more of the same length before calling it a day.

Later, Kurensky stressed the importance of not playing a shot until Faldo was absolutely ready to do so.

'Never play when you're not 100 per cent sure it's going to come off. There's an element of doubt and that kills it,' Kurensky told Faldo. 'You must be positive, confident of what you're going to do. When you get a bad lie or a difficult shot accept it as an opportunity to show your potential. Don't think to yourself: "This is difficult, I'm in danger of fluffing it." Show off. Let everybody see it's a tough shot and then they'll think you're a miracle-maker.'

Kurensky laid down other rules she wanted Faldo to follow and gave them to him, typewritten on three sheets of paper. It was his list of do's and don'ts:

● Never change your mind unless it is because you haven't assessed the situation properly. In that case you're not demonstrating indecision. You're making sure you have gathered the information on which to base your assessment of the situation.

● Always maintain your cause position. Don't become affected by anything which happens to you which you don't like. Just say to yourself 'What is my intention? My intention is to win.'

● Warm up mentally as well as physically. If you hit a good three-iron shot and then another, stop after that. You can't do any better than that so put the club away and forget about it. Take another club out and hit with that. If you keep hitting shots with one club you are weakening your mental powers.

● Look at difficult situations. Don't run away from them. Don't get depressed. Don't take chances. Remain cool and then decide the best course of action. Never take a risk.

● Your best golf will materialise when you swing smoothly with natural rhythm and no forcing.

The best example of Faldo's improved mental approach came on the third day of the tournament. He was playing well and lying second to Ballesteros when he ran into trouble on the eighth and took a three over par seven. He stormed onto the next tee and said to his caddie, Dave McNeilly, 'That's it, Dave. I've had enough. Give me a wedge. I'm going to hole it. I can see it clearly.' Faldo concentrated hard and just before he hit the ball he said quietly to himself, under his breath: 'Come on. Give me a ten. As the ball flew away he thought he'd done it. The ball looked as though it was going to end in the hole. It bounced on the green, bit into the turf and came to a halt two feet from the flag. A birdie was a formality. Then Faldo birdied the next hole as well. By the end of the tournament, Faldo, not dithering over club selection and following Kurensky's instructions as best he could, had finished in second place. Seve Ballesteros was a runaway winner by five shots. As evidence of the effectiveness of

Kurensky's teaching this result was inconclusive. Faldo, after all, had been in second place when she gave him her advice, and she did not – as she had promised she would – make him 'win the tournament'. Faldo himself, however, felt that she had helped him.

The man who came last was South African Denis Watson, who, despite this showing, was a spectacular example of what mental training can do for a golfer. Since July 1984 when he had begun working with Dr Robert Rotella, a sports psychologist at the University of Virginia, Watson had been transformed. Up to July he had only once, in the first seven months of the year, finished in the top ten of a tournament in the US. But from July to October he improved so much that he won three tournaments and $350,000. This surge in the second half of the season all but gave him the coveted Player of the Year award in the US. It was, however, won by his namesake Tom Watson for the sixth time in eight years.

'Bob doesn't just teach me positive thinking,' Watson told me. 'It's much more a case of turning negatives into positives.' In a recent round he had been going along very nicely and was three under par. Then he took a horrible double bogey. 'I hadn't missed a shot all day to that point. But instead of thinking about that double bogey as I once would have done, I concentrated on remembering how well I was hitting the ball the rest of the time. As a result I played great on the back nine. I could have birdied almost every hole.'

Rotella works intensively for up to fourteen hours each day. Then he gives each client a three-page checklist to read last thing at night. Watson's takes him no more than ten minutes. By the time he starts reading it he has already spent an hour reviewing his round and imagining himself hitting one good shot after another. Each morning he tries to get himself into a frame of mind he refers to as The Zone – a state of calm confidence where he believes he can't do anything wrong. He reached The Zone briefly during the World Series tournament in Ohio in August 1984 and thanks to a stunning 62 he won the event. He found The Zone again a few weeks later when he had five birdies in six holes on his way to victory in a tournament in Las Vegas. He was so confident that day that even when faced with a shot requiring a carry of 240 yards over water and into a wind, he had no hesitation in going for it. 'It never occurred to me not to go for it. I knew I could make it.'

Rotella is a three-handicap golfer who was already working with the American star Tom Kite when Watson became a client. 'A lot of people think I've been teaching Denis to go out and kill everybody. I spend a lot of time telling him you don't have to have a killer instinct. You have to learn to get out of your own way and instead of being your own worst enemy become your own best friend.

'The people I work with are very talented athletes,' Rotella continued. 'But somewhere along the line they have been led to feel inferior. Denis had all kinds of confidence at some point in his life but somewhere he threw it away. Some of it had to do with coming to the US and being intimidated after hearing how great the American players were.'

This struck a chord with Faldo. It had been a problem he wanted help with after he had first been to the US and it was something he asked Sherno about when they began working together in 1982. Faldo wanted to know what it would be like to be under pressure in the US and how to cope with it. He was keen to learn how to deal with noisy American crowds. What struck Sherno was Faldo's willingness to adapt to doing things the American way. 'He wasn't one of those Brits who says, "That isn't the way we do it back home." He was willing to play it on their terms and that struck me as smart.'

To improve Faldo's concentration Sherno would shout out, 'Good shot' as Faldo was beginning his downswing. The first time this completely threw him and he dropped the club and started laughing. Soon he learned to ignore it. Sherno also helped Faldo come to terms with bad shots. 'What happens when you don't get the result you want?' he asked Faldo. 'You are aiming to hit the ball on to the green and four feet from the flag and in fact it winds up under a tree. Just give it a number. You can't bullshit too much about numbers. You say to yourself, "I planned a nine and I got a four. So what? Big deal. You want to get angry about that? You want to make yourself tense and upset yourself. Go ahead if you want to but you don't have to." I was trying to give him a technique that would be better than the conditioning he had been using for years, which was that if he hit a bad shot he punished himself. I was trying to teach him how to forgive himself. We called it letting go of the mistake. He recognised that the Americans had that capacity and he wanted it because he reckoned it would stand him in good stead.'

Sherno noticed, from reading newspaper stories and watching television, a significant improvement in Faldo's mental approach over the years. He noticed that Faldo didn't get so steamed up over bad shots, a habit that was pronounced when he first turned pro, as he once had, and that he could still rise to the occasion beautifully. 'Being able to get yourself into optimum condition without help from anyone, not from your caddie nor from anyone in the gallery, is the sign of a person who is in the top division,' says Sherno. 'Nick has that capacity, there's no question of that.'

Faldo set off for the States at the start of 1985 with his hopes high, based on what he had learned from Kurensky, though he was also honest enough to admit he found it hard to remember all the instructions she had given to him. 'There's no way you can correctly assess every single situation,' he said before he left. 'If you could do that then somebody would have done it already and you'd have had scores in the fifties. If I could put this sort of power into my golf for five hours then I'd be unbeatable. But your mind must wander because you're only human. The bottom line is that no matter how much she tells me it is still down to me. She can give me all the information, but if I have no will to go out and do it then it's no good.'

Faldo brightened for a moment as he thought of another aspect of the routines. 'The most wonderful thing is that you forget the golf swing. You don't think to yourself, "I've got to cock my left wrist, take it back this way, make sure it's all right at the top." All you're trying to do is to hit that ball from A to B and get a result. That's the best bit. It's fantastic.'

That Faldo had been prepared to work first with Sherno and then Kurensky was revealing, for he has the average person's uneasiness concerning matters to do with the mind. To him, it was something you didn't discuss, like sex or politics and if you had to talk about sports psychologists then you tended to use the pejorative term 'trick cyclist'. 'Frankly I was embarrassed when the subject first came up,' Faldo recalls. 'I thought it was something to do with lying on a couch talking to a man with a torch on his head asking you what's going on in your mind. I was a bit scared he would turn me into a freak.'

But Faldo is more prepared than most golfers to do anything to improve his game. I recall an afternoon I spent with him at Royal St George's golf course in Kent before the 1981 Open. I walked out through a heat haze towards the second green where Faldo, his caddie Andy Prodger and a friend of Faldo's were at work. Prodger was striding from the flag to one corner of the green, pacing off a long putt. His baggy brown trousers looked, as usual, as though they were about to fall down. Faldo was standing behind a bunker looking first at the sand beneath his feet and then glancing at the flag. His friend was pulling a measuring wheel from a knoll in the fairway fifty yards short of the green to where Faldo's big blue bag was resting on the edge of the green.

It was the same at the next hole and the hole after that. Detail, detail, detail. He often threw three balls into a bunker to attempt recovery shots. He made dozens of measurements and jotted them down in a notebook. From the tees of the short holes he would hit at least two different irons. The round took nearly six hours and by the end of it I was impressed by Faldo's attention to detail. He had left nothing to chance.

For a while I thought this zealousness was only sporadic and that he had laid it on a bit at St George's. Then I noticed that he was as thorough in France, in Spain, in America, in Scotland. He played a practice round with Morris Hatalsky before the 1984 Open at St Andrews. It was Hatalsky's first sight of the fabled Old Course, but it was Faldo who lingered on each green practising putting at different targets and who sometimes hit two or three shots to a green.

To my mind Faldo is just about the most single-minded player on the European tour. Would anyone else cut their finger nails only on a Monday lest the sensitivity of their hands on the putter handle be disrupted? This sort of attention to detail comes from an all-consuming desire to improve and the way he thinks about tournaments bears out those words spoken by his headmaster twenty years ago: 'I don't know what he is going to do . . . but I'm certain he'll do it well.' There are other aspects to Faldo that set him apart. He is brisk and businesslike, a scholar moving up the class, and he doesn't haunt the bar or fool around with friends on the putting green. He is often on his own and is known as a loner by the other pros.

'Some players moan and groan and say, "Faldo doesn't want to talk to anybody, he practises all the time, he's a boring person,"' says Ronan Rafferty, the young professional. 'The guy wants to be a great player. You can't take it away from him that he has gone ahead and done his own thing. He has cut out all the bullshit and gone and won. That's what we all dream of doing. Frankly, I'm as jealous as hell.'

His reputation as a loner dates back to his early days as a pro. Like most struggling young players he had to watch his budget carefully. He was not extravagant in his personal tastes and he ate well but inexpensively. He did, however, insist on having his own room. 'When I started touring my father said to me, "If we can afford it you'd do better having a room on your own." So I did, right from the start. I didn't worry about that from the money point of view. I didn't want to have to worry about trying to get to sleep if my roommate didn't also want to go to sleep and I certainly didn't want to be woken up if somebody else was getting up early. I decided it would be better for my golf if I didn't share. That's how I came to be labelled as a loner.'

Not entirely joking, Faldo's mother used to say, 'Nick's different, he's special,' from the time he was born. His parents scrimped and saved to get him anything he wanted – bicycles, canoe, golf equipment, tennis rackets. At times it seemed as though nothing was too good for him. As a result this instilled great confidence into Faldo. He felt they were proud of him and it became natural for him to hold his head up high and to think of himself as someone special.

Thinking like this, he didn't regard it as unusual that when he turned pro he wanted to show how much he believed in himself by starting without any sponsorship. He and his father turned down several offers from would-be backers who were attracted by Faldo's brilliant amateur career.

'If you're confident and you know you're going to make it then you don't want the guy from down the road knocking on your front door saying: "Remember me? I lent you £20,000 to play the tour and you've only repaid me £15,000. Now you've won £100,000 I want twenty-five per cent of that. It's in the contract."' Faldo then said something very revealing: 'That may be all right for the guy who hasn't got any ambition. He thinks, "Great, somebody is paying my expenses and I'm able to concentrate on the tour." But to my mind that's not breeding a champion. I'm advocating that kids should struggle a bit and trust their own ability for a while and stay independent.'

Faldo's single-mindedness and hard work, not to mention his confidence in himself, paid off in his first full season as a pro. It's accepted on the tour that amateurs who have just turned pro take a while to find their feet, get used to the higher standard of play, learn the art of scoring when not playing well. Faldo made the change from amateur to pro so successfully that by the end of 1977, his first full season, he lay eighth in the money list. He had won two tournaments, finished second in another and accumulated £23,000. Rookie pros just aren't supposed to do that. Tony Jacklin didn't, nor did Peter Oosterhuis, nor did Greg Norman. The only player who has matched it is Gordon Brand Junior in 1982.

Faldo doesn't have Greg Norman's exuberant manner, or Tony Jacklin's confident air. In character he is more like Seve Ballesteros and Bernhard Langer, his rivals. Though these three have different backgrounds, nationalities, languages and even physiques, they have in common single-mindedness and an enormous belief in their own golfing ability.

Faldo has never allowed himself to be overawed by anyone since the day he, an unknown amateur from Hertfordshire, met John Davies, a British international, in The Amateur in June 1975. 'I thought to myself, "If I beat this guy I'll make a name for myself." I wasn't scared of him. He had it all to lose, I had it all to gain. I just went out and duffed him up.'

Boastful or glib as that may sound, it's no less than what happened on that occasion, and Faldo has been able to summon up this irreverence for apparent elders and betters at different times throughout his career, the most famous occasion being the last day's singles of the 1977 Ryder Cup. Faldo, a pro for a mere seventeen months, faced Tom Watson, who had won his second Open just two months earlier. They came to the 18th tee all square. Showing poise and skill beyond his years, Faldo parred the hole for victory. 'To my mind the strength of Nick's game has been that he felt he could win in any company,' says John Jacobs, who was later to captain two Ryder Cup sides in which Faldo played. 'When I first met and talked to Nick it was obvious that he wasn't a particularly good swinger. But he didn't know that. He thought he was ever so good and therefore he aimed high internationally. Since Tony Jacklin we haven't had any British players other than Peter Oosterhuis who thought big enough. I think that as long ago as 1978 and 1979 Nick was thinking he could win the Open, could win in America.

'I have seen him on the first tee on major occasions and he is totally in control of himself,' continues Jacobs. 'He is trying to win the Open from the first shot, as opposed to hoping to do well. A lot of people will say to you, "I'm not just playing to do well, I'm playing to win," and you know damn well they're kidding themselves and trying to kid you. In Faldo's case you can see that he is the other way around. He is not there just to play well in it. He's there to try and win it.'

If you examine Faldo's career you will notice that he always seemed to know what was best for him and his golf. He chose to stay with Dave McNeilly, his caddie, when he could have had his pick of a dozen others, and has now been proved right. It was he, with some help from his father, who decided to quit Houston University after less than three months, a decision that was criticised at first in some quarters. Again, Faldo was proved right. And after his early success as a pro in Europe, he declined to rush off to the US until he'd had a thorough grounding in Europe first of all. Indeed the failure of his marriage could be the exception that proves the general rule that Faldo knows what's best for him.

It's this down-to-earth, realistic side to his nature that prevents him from having many superstitions. He does insist on the coins that he uses as ball markers having low dates (1968) rather than high dates (1979) in the hope that they will inspire him to shoot 68's rather than 79's. In the first round of the 1983 Open at Birkdale he took a six on each of the two opening holes, thereby squandering four strokes to par. The ball he was using was a Titleist bearing the number one. It was nearly two years before he could bring himself to use a Titleist one again.

But such superstitions as these, if indeed they can even be called superstitions, don't bear comparison with those of some of his colleagues. Seve Ballesteros, for example, always wears something blue on the last day of a tournament. For years Tony Jacklin banned green from his wardrobe after he'd had anything but the luck of the Irish one day and shot an 82. Even the great Jack Nicklaus, as strong-willed a competitor as there has ever been in golf, believes he is brought luck by always wearing a white golf glove on his left hand, white golf shoes and carrying the same three pennies and metal gadget with which to repair the pitch marks of a ball on the green. And he may be right. After losing the ball-mark repairer on the eve of the 1984 US PGA championship, Nicklaus had to play without it for the first time for twenty years – and went perilously close to missing the cut.

Faldo has something of the gilded youth about him, a convincing air that is intimidating to rivals. His clothes are well cut and brightly-coloured. Even in a high wind or heavy rain he seems to get less windblown and wet than anybody else. He walks briskly between shots and his swing is so rhythmical and easy to watch that you'd be forgiven for thinking that hitting a golf ball is a piece of cake.

All this breeds resentment; it would be silly to claim that it doesn't. Faldo isn't the most popular player on the tour, any more than he has enjoyed a perfectly harmonious relationship with the press. But he has begun to repair his image. He doesn't like being described as a loner, partly because he isn't really and partly because he has feelings like anybody else and would prefer that his fellow players, and the press, thought of him as an easy-going, uncomplicated bloke. But he is pragmatic about it and if this is the reputation he gets from his determination to become a better golfer then he isn't going to lose any sleep over it. He will simply work harder than ever and become more determined to succeed.

'Few would touch Nick for work,' says Rafferty. 'If you ever want to know where Nick is, then start looking on the practice ground. He wants to work on his golf longer than anybody else wants to work on theirs. When he practises his putting he isn't satisfied with a few putts. He goes out, has six fifteen-ft putts and stands there until he has holed them all. I remember sitting on a bench by the putting green at Sunningdale watching Nick. As soon as he missed one putt he started his routine all over again. When he got out onto the course the putts were going in as they had on the putting green.'

No one has ever accused Faldo of not devoting the maximum effort to his golf. It's striking how successfully he makes sure that golf always comes first, before any other commitments. 'Whereas after a round most people will grab their wives and say, "Come on, let's go back to the hotel," Nick says he is going to practise,' points out Rafferty. 'He will practise, then go to the putting green, do some chipping and bunker shots and then fiddle about a bit more. He'd make sure his business was done first before he cared for anybody else's.' He's no different in this from Langer or Ballesteros.

Because hard work, single-mindedness and determination have worked so well for Faldo he believes they would also work as well for others, if only they would put their minds to it. 'There are a few young golfers in Europe who have it in them to become good players,' says Faldo. 'I'm thinking of Paul Way, Mike McLean, Roger Chapman. I looked at Roger and thought, "It's all there, he's a helluva player." He just needs to believe in himself. I think he's lacking that little something. He needs to get mad with himself sometimes.

'It's all a matter of how determined you are, how committed you are to devoting your life to golf. If you do this and you become successful then you run the risk of your mates saying to you: "You're not part of our happy group on tour any more." But if you really have the desire to be a good player then you will move on and find new mates anyway. Your new mates will be Tom Watson and the like.'

Faldo is alert and anxious to try any development or trend that may help him to improve – and not just his golf swing either. Since he read a book called **Eat to Win**, written by nutritionist Robert Haas, who has advised Martina Navratilova, he has cut out soft drinks and dark meat in favour of chicken, fish and pasta. He noticed that Jack Nicklaus carries apples or bananas around in his bag, so now each morning Dave McNeilly brings some from a local fruiterer. Faldo drinks at most two beers each day; he abhors smoking. When he is at home he runs two or three miles every other day. He won't do any weight training, saying it would make him too muscular. And he's not even prepared to enter the **Superstars** competition on television, despite their repeated attempts to lure him on to it, because his competitive instinct would make sure he did some specific training for it and such training would develop the wrong muscles.

On both Nick Faldo and Denis Watson the jury are still out, considering their verdict. Faldo is not a one-season wonder as we may yet come to describe Watson, though that is unlikely. But how Faldo develops in the coming years depends on how badly he wants to develop. Years ago he improved by leaps and bounds; now his improvement is measured in inches. This may be appropriate for, as someone once said, the most important inches are those between the ears. Has Faldo reached his potential? I don't think so, not by a long chalk. But if he is to improve from now on it will be as a result of working as hard with his mind as he once did with his swing.

CHAPTER 7

The Swing

Golf would be easy if we could walk into a sports shop and say: 'I'd like a golf swing please.'

'Certainly sir,' the assistant would reply. 'Which one would you like? You're a tall man, you look as though you could handle the Peter Oosterhuis model. It's a bit unreliable on the driving I'm afraid, inclined to push the odd shot. But it's mustard around the greens.

'If that one doesn't suit you I can offer you our Brian Barnes model. It's very sturdy. I've sold more of that model than any other over the years and no one has ever come back and complained about it. It's on special offer this week. We've knocked off ten per cent already and we might be able to do a little better if you were really interested.'

Unfortunately, we can't do that. The idea of being able to buy a golf swing, attractive as it may seem, is far removed from reality, which is that a swing is developed by hours of hard work and shaped to suit a person's height, weight, suppleness, strength and a dozen other characteristics. It can be complex as is Bobby Clampett's. He says he has twenty-four check points to tick off in his mind before he can hit a ball. Or it can be natural and rhythmical, no more complicated than swishing at tufts of grass on an afternoon walk.

Nick Faldo's long and languid swing belongs in this latter

category, but this is the result of many hours spent building it up layer by layer, testing, experimenting and refining at each stage before moving on.

The man who drummed the initial thoughts concerning the golf swing into Faldo's head was Chris Arnold, the assistant pro at Welwyn Garden City Golf Club. Faldo's mother had taken him there, having booked a course of lessons some weeks previously. Keen as Faldo was, at first he was not allowed to do anything more than learn how to grip a club, to stand correctly and to make a few tentative swishes. These were fundamentals that Arnold believed in, as did his boss Ian Connelly, the pro at the golf club who was soon to take over from Arnold as Faldo's teacher.

Connelly was a Scot who had learned much of his instruction technique while he was assistant to Jimmy Adams at Royal Mid-Surrey. He believed in getting the fundamentals right – the grip, the set-up and the posture. As he wrote later in **Golf World**, 'Why start off your golfing career with a bad grip which will require compensations? Grip properly and other facets of your swing will more readily fit into place.

'I believe in young players developing good habits from the word go, which will stand them in good stead later and make their development as players easier. A good swing is built around a good grip.'

Connelly made sure that Faldo placed his hands on the club in such a way that they and the clubface were in the same position at the set-up as at impact. He wanted what he called neutrality in Faldo's grip – for it to be neither too strong nor too weak. From the start Faldo used the overlapping grip, named after the famed professional Harry Vardon. In this he was like most golfers, though not Jack Nicklaus who preferred the interlocking grip. In the interlocking grip the little finger of the right hand is tucked into the space between the index and middle finger of the left hand. Nicklaus has explained many times that his hands, which have small and chubby fingers, felt more compact this way. Faldo's hands gave no cause for concern in this department. The palms were the size of plates; the fingers as long as a concert pianist's.

(As it happened Faldo's contemporary Sandy Lyle spent the first twenty years of his golfing career with an overlapping grip. Then in the autumn of 1984, while practising one day, he started to experiment with an interlocking grip. He loved it immediately. He found his right hand wasn't so dominant in his swing, that he had less trouble getting the ball into the air, that his new grip gave him more touch in his short game and that he hit the ball further. Over the next few weeks he had sudden and dramatic proof of its efficiency when he won more than £200,000 in prize money from three tournaments.)

Just as Connelly wanted as few potential errors as possible in Faldo's grip, so he ordained that his pupil's set-up should be as near as possible the same as at the moment of impact. 'Peter Thomson's philosophy is that the swing is very simple and I agree with him,' says Connelly. 'The best swing is the most simple swing. It cuts down on mistakes.'

Following these instructions was not particularly difficult for Faldo. He was an excellent listener and a hard worker. He did as he was told when he had lessons with Connelly and then he went off and practised for hours by himself. The trouble began with his posture. He was tall for his age and like many tall men he tended to stand too near the ball. This made him stoop when Connelly wanted him to be slightly tilted from the waist, with just enough clearance for the backswing and downswing. To be poised, nicely balanced, like a cat about to spring, was how Connelly would describe it.

As a result of standing too close to the ball, Faldo tended to take his club back rather steeply and so at the top of the backswing he had to drop his hands inside to get them into the right position. This maneouvre looked at times like a flail and at times like a loop and it was to be some years before he got rid of it completely.

In 1974 Faldo went with his father to the Open at Royal Lytham. They stayed for the week and Faldo spent most of the time watching competitors on the practice ground, scoring the rhythm of their swings into his memory. This helped him find his own rhythm and it was beneficial later when he needed to produce a shot of a certain shape. If faced with a shot needing a slight fade then Faldo summoned up an image of Johnny Miller's swing on the practice ground at Lytham. If a draw was called for he used what he described as his Tom Weiskopf swing. And for a slice the only swing he needed to picture in his mind's eye was Lee Trevino's.

In general, at this time Faldo modelled his swing on Jerry Heard, the young American pro. 'I thought his swing was fantastic,' Faldo recalls. 'He had a short backswing and superb rhythm. Everything was clean and crisp.' Faldo was still in this Jerry Heard swing phase when he was invited to play golf with Mark McCormack at Sunningdale. McCormack wanted to cast an eye over the highly praised amateur he had been told about. During their round McCormack remarked to Faldo: 'You know Nick, your swing reminds me awfully of Jerry Heard's.' Faldo was tickled pink at hearing that. He couldn't have been given a better compliment.

Conventional wisdom is that it is sensible to encourage young players to learn to play with only a few clubs at first, no more than a half set, so they learn to hit shots of different length and shape with one club. Faldo disagrees with this view. 'I don't think that early on it would have benefited me,' he says. 'I wouldn't have known what I was teaching myself. On the other hand it would be beneficial for me now to practise and play with only a few clubs. It might teach me some imagination. I think that pros get very stuck with yardage charts and things.'

Ask any pro what is Faldo's greatest asset and the chances

are he will say Faldo's rhythm. 'He's got the best rhythm I think I've ever seen,' says Roger Chapman. Faldo's ability to swing so smoothly is a gift, there's no doubt about that, but since he discovered that he had it he has worked hard on maintaining it. Connelly recalls a conversation with Faldo. 'Today's lesson is about tempo,' Connelly said. 'What's tempo?' Faldo asked. Connelly explained by saying something to the effect that it was the speed at which a person felt comfortable when he was swinging a club, when the club was in control. It was not a set speed that a teacher could lay down. 'It would be something like one, two, three and then hit the ball,' Connelly said, being as vague as he could be because he wasn't sure how to define it himself, and he didn't want to do anything to disturb Faldo's natural rhythm.

More than once when they were together on a practice ground they did an experiment to prove that rhythm was more important in the golf swing than strength. Connelly would throw down a dozen balls and a challenge: 'Go on Nick. Hit those as if your life depended on them. Give them everything you've got. Jump out of your shoes as you make contact.' Faldo would do as he was bidden, grunting with the effort, and they would record where the balls landed.

Then Connelly would throw down another dozen balls and this time say, 'Nick, I want you to hit these really slowly, concentrating on your rhythm.' Faldo would begin and within moments these balls would be flying as far as those from the first group.

Roger Chapman remembers seeing Faldo on a practice ground, hitting driver shots. Everything looked normal to Chapman until he realised that Faldo's shots were going no further than 180 yards. 'He was rehearsing his rhythm,' says Chapman.

In his garage Faldo keeps a Spalding driver to which he has added lead taken from fishing weights. Since the weight is all in one place, the club feels extraordinarily heavy. In fact it is no more than twice the weight of Faldo's regular MacGregor driver. To make sure he swings at the correct tempo Faldo likes to spend time swinging this club. On one occasion he thought he had lost his rhythm and in an attempt to regain it he swung his weighted driver for twenty minutes each day – but without gripping with the thumb and index finger of his right hand. 'If I squeezed with my thumb and index finger I found that I was putting pressure on the muscles on the top of my right forearm and this, I felt, would encourage me to come over the top of the ball in my downswing' says Faldo. 'If, however, I use only the last three fingers then this pulls the muscles **under** my right forearm and this in turn prompts me to get my hands into the ball correctly – and without any danger of my coming over the top.'

As he grew up Faldo was one of a group of young golfers of similar age who played and practised at Welwyn Garden City Golf Club. John Moorhouse, later to be Faldo's tour caddie, and his brother Colin were two, and Trevor Powell, who turned pro just before Faldo, was a third. They played games among themselves, throwing each other's golf balls into the bushes by the side of the practice green to see who could get the ball out and into the hole in the fewest strokes.

When he wasn't playing games like this Faldo was often to be seen hitting hundreds of balls down the 17th fairway, keeping an eye open for members going up the 11th, because he knew then that he had only an hour or so before they would arrive on the 17th tee. And in lulls between lessons and games with his contemporaries Faldo would spend time swinging a club in the long grass at one end of the practice ground using either his left hand or both his hands. His strong right arm didn't need strengthening he had decided. For a while he used a wrist exerciser and then he went through a phase of doing press-ups. He abandoned both when he discovered that the best way of strengthening his muscles for golf was by playing, practising and using that weighted club.

Meanwhile he wasn't ignoring his putting. He developed a stroke of his own, one that he could repeat effortlessly. It was tested once and it was discovered that he hit every putt with his putter blade opened by a half degree. As champions are supposed to, Faldo would spend hours putting on the carpets at home. The hall carpet was textured and quite bumpy. A Persian rug elsewhere in the house was smoother and faster. In those days Faldo says that the fastest greens in the area were at Knebworth Golf Club near Stevenage and when he was going to play there he would put in several extra putting sessions at home, this time on the fastest surface he could find: the linoleum on the kitchen floor. 'I took a backswing of one inch to hit the ball a few feet,' he says, a smile appearing on his face at the memory. 'It was great practice. By the time I had done that for half an hour I was able to make a three-inch backswing so controlled I needed only to touch the ball to start it rolling.

'In those days I could hole anything,' says Faldo. 'I really could putt then. We used to play on the putting green for a Mars bar or something like that. Give me one opportunity to catch up if I was down, or to hole a long putt for victory and it always went in. Never mind how difficult the putt was I always sank it. In those days I really could see the ball going into the hole. That was the way to do it. You never hole a putt by standing there thinking, "I've got to do this, I've got to do that". You've got to see the ball go into the hole and then it just happens. I had no fear in those days, whereas I have now. Fear comes with age unfortunately. I've seen a few too many putts miss at crucial stages.'

Time and again during their lessons Connelly would stress that he wanted Faldo's swing to be an American one, in which he didn't stoop too much, turned fully on the backswing and powered through the ball. 'Ian told me that all great swings were short and solid,' says Faldo. 'He didn't want mine to be long and loose.' It was hard for Faldo though. He was naturally supple and because of the steepness of his backswing things went wrong at the top. Faldo was gifted but not a particularly good striker, thought John Jacobs, the eminent golf teacher, seeing Faldo for the first time. 'His swing was not as good as it looked,' says Jacobs. 'He was tall, handsome and he had a good rhythm. But he used to swing back too straight and therefore his shoulders rocked in sympathy with that swing path. When he swung back so straight his right side didn't get out of the way on the backswing and his left side was in the way on the downswing. Thus he pushed some shots and hooked others.'

This fault tended to create others, one of which was a tendency to counter his hook by aiming left in order to encourage himself to swing across the ball and thus fade it. A quick lesson in alignment given to Faldo by Jacobs on the morning of the last day of the 1981 Ryder Cup made all the difference in that day's singles. Faldo went out and defeated Johnny Miller 2 and 1.

To try and cure Faldo's tendency to stoop Connelly told him to practise by raising the club a foot or so off the ground and then swinging. This helped to flatten out his steep arc. It's a routine that tall golfers like Peter Oosterhuis and Andy North use as well. When they were practising together Connelly would make Faldo address a ball and then press the shaft of a club against Faldo's right arm to make sure that he began his backswing with the clubhead first and not the arms.

Yet even when Faldo was devoting hours to improving his swing bad habits crept in unnoticed and it took his fellow pros to point them out to him. Playing a practice round with Faldo before the Open at Troon, Watson encouraged the Englishman to move his left arm forward at the address so that the arm and the clubhead were more in line. Faldo was warming up before another tournament when North stopped to have a look. After a moment or two he rapped Faldo's right foot with the head of his driver. 'Get it back,' said the 1978 US Open champion. Faldo moved the offending object. 'More,' snapped North. Faldo shuffled a little more.

'Come on Nick,' said North, a note of exasperation entering his voice. 'Move it or I'll crack it with this club.' Finally Faldo had got his right toe back into a position that satisfied North. 'I was in the habit of turning it too far towards my target,' Faldo explains. 'So it was restricting my turn.'

At the age of forty, Jack Nicklaus decided that the swing he had first learned as a boy under the keen eye of Jack Grout was no longer working as well as it should have been. By Nicklaus's own high standards, 1979 had been a very poor year. So he decided to rebuild his swing, which he did with hours of work between January and May of 1980. The result must have exceeded his wildest dreams. He went on to win the US Open and the US PGA, the first time since 1975 that he had won two major events in one season. There is a lesson there for Faldo and lesser golfers – if Nicklaus hasn't stopped learning about the swing then they shouldn't think they have either.

Nevertheless, Faldo does sometimes wonder whether anything else can go wrong with his swing that hasn't already occurred. 'I think I've had everything that could go wrong,' he says. 'Locking the left knee, too long a backswing, turning too much, not turning enough. Once I used my legs too much, then I went through a period of not using them enough. Sometimes I stand too open, sometimes too shut. I have a tendency to come over the top. I've had a loop. I've let go of the club at the top of the backswing. I stoop. You name it, I've had it.' As he encountered each of these ailments Faldo felt increasing frustration. He began to wonder if there would ever be an end to them all. Then he realised that he could benefit and learn from them. He tried out corrective techniques and watched to see if they worked. Each time one did he felt happier. He was learning not only what caused his mistakes but how to cure them.

By the start of 1983 Faldo's swing was very much as it is today. He had overcome any tendency to stoop. His leg action was good. His loop had gone. All that remained was the occasional practice of dragging shots to the left, which he was able to overcome with help from his friend Mark O'Meara, and a lingering looseness at the top of the backswing. Try as he might he couldn't eradicate this flaw completely. In the end he found a cure for it, fortuitously. He was on a practice ground next to Seve Ballesteros and his caddie for that tournament, Dave Musgrove, himself a useful player, was commenting on the smoothness and firmness of Seve's swing.

'That's what you've got to get your swing like, Nick,' said Musgrove. 'You've got to tighten it up a bit.' 'I'm trying to but I can't,' Faldo replied. 'I'll go and ask Seve,' said Musgrove. 'You look so solid at the top of the backswing, how do you do it?' Musgrove asked the man for whom he had caddied at Lytham in 1979. 'Is eassy,' Ballesteros said in a shower of sibilant sounds. 'Put more pressure on the left thumb.' Faldo was dumbstruck, partly with embarrassment at not having thought of that himself. 'Of course,' he said as he tried it out. 'How obvious!'

When that flaw was corrected Faldo made his swing about as good as he could, as good, Chapman believes, as those of Ballesteros and Sam Torrance who, in his view, are the two best swingers in Europe. 'I'm happy with Nick's swing now he has his alignment sorted out,' says Jacobs. 'He very rarely plays badly.'

Yet there is one area where Faldo feels inadequate and that is his ability to visualise an unusual shot. 'It's what Seve has. He pictures a shot and then he plays it and it's totally different from the shot you're thinking of. Years ago at the Laurent Perrier he had missed a green to the left. The pin was left and he had a big bunker to go over. I thought he would take his sand wedge, flick the ball up in the air and hope it would stop by the flag. What does he do? He takes out a putter, goes whack so that his ball races through the bunker, hops up over the lip and ends four feet from the hole. Where did that shot come from? He just dreams them up.

'I remember Trevino playing a brilliant shot at Augusta,' Faldo continued. 'He had driven his ball too far left on the second and as the pin was back left he was stuck. He had to hit an iron short and lay up. Then I looked back and saw he had a three wood in his hand and I thought to myself, "Oh boy, he doesn't know what he's doing. Watch out gallery." Trevino went down the grip and deliberately hit a duck hook that landed short, raced through the bunker because of the spin and ended fifteen feet away. He holed it for a three.'

Throughout 1984 Faldo seemed unsettled as he addressed the ball, something noticed by the professional Chris Moody when they played together in South Africa in December. 'He does look a bit edgy and when it gets tense this may find him out,' says Moody 'but I know he's working on it.' In recent times the most notable example of fidgeting is Mark James who, for a while, went through a ritual of gripping and regripping his club twenty or more times before hitting the ball. Faldo is not as bad as that but before playing that brilliant seven iron shot on the fifteenth at the Heritage he did the following: stepped up to the ball right foot first; flicked his trousers with his left hand; brought up his left foot to the address; lifted his club while adjusting his feet to the required line; dropped the club behind the ball; looked to his left at the target; lifted the club again; looked left again; lowered the club; shifted his feet; raised the club; moved it three or four feet back from the ball along the path he wanted it to go during the swing; waggled it three more times; shuffled his feet three more times; then swung at the ball.

'Golfers do fidget,' says Peter McEvoy, the distinguished

amateur. 'It comes and it goes. I had a stage once when I couldn't take the club away from the ball. Another time I always seemed to have a stiffness in my neck. They were both idiosyncracies and they didn't last long. Rituals like this look worse than they are.'

'There was a time when Nick got the clubhead into rather a shut position at the top of the backswing,' says Michael King, the Ryder Cup player. 'He has improved that now. He has his swing much more on line and he points the clubhead at the target at the top of the backswing. Yet all the time he was trying to get the plane of his swing right he was saved by his rhythm. It helped him maintain his form. His rhythm is second to none.

'Nick is strong, one of the strongest chaps on the tour, and terribly, terribly good at keeping the clubhead totally under control. He has never hit **at** a ball in his life. Have you ever seen him smack **at** a ball? Of course you haven't. Even when he gets hot he doesn't change his swing, his tempo. Look at some players and notice how they quicken up or slow down according to how they're playing. Nick has never had that problem. He is so level-headed as far as golfing brains are concerned, he has managed to keep his swing as slow as possible.

'Tom Watson has a faster rhythm and other people swing slower than Nick. But with Nick you can see as he takes the club back that there is going to be so much time for him to do whatever he wants to do.' King paused and then concluded, with more than a hint of admiration in his voice, 'His rhythm is the best I've ever seen.'

CHAPTER 8

LEGACY – The Open

If Nick Faldo is to win the Open, as he is perfectly capable of doing, then he will have to shoulder aside some of the large historical boulders that stand in his way at present. Only ten British or Irish golfers have won an Open since 1914 and, if we exclude a flurry of home players who won immediately after the war, then the gap between victories has been widening: three years between George Duncan in 1920 and Arthur Havers; eleven between Havers and Cotton's first; eighteen from Faulkner's victory in the only Open ever held in Ireland until Tony Jacklin's at Royal Lytham in 1969. That span of eighteen years is the longest time in the history of the Open to have passed without a home victory.

Year after year thousands of spectators flock to the Open, one of Europe's biggest sporting occasions, only to see their hopes of a home victory dashed just as they are, as often as not, in the Wimbledon tennis championships, which by tradition precede the Open. Over the years there have been some heroic attempts at victory: Syd Scott and Dai Rees just being edged out by Peter Thomson at Royal Birkdale in 1954; David Thomas, said to be the longest straight driver in the world at the time, being beaten in a play-off in 1958; and Thomas again getting to within one stroke of Jack Nicklaus in the last round at Muirfield in 1966. For five years out of six starting in 1967 even Tony Jacklin, who did win in 1969, was destined to do no better than third.

This bleak picture continued through the nineteen seventies and may have reached its peak in 1982 when five players from Britain or Ireland were all in contention on the last day. Des Smyth, an Irishman, the Scots Sandy Lyle (who was born in England) and Sam Torrance and Nick Faldo and his fellow Englishman Peter Oosterhuis, who had lived in the US for nearly ten years, all got close to the title. But in the end they all fell short, as did Nick Price of Zimbabwe and, to his surprise, Tom Watson won his fourth Open.

Players from these islands have led after the first round, the second round and the third round of different Opens. A number have even gone very close to taking the glittering prize: Dai Rees at Birkdale (1961), Christy O'Connor and Brian Huggett on the same course four years later and Peter Oosterhuis at both Lytham in 1974 and Troon in 1982 all finished second. Over the years, and excepting the glorious victory by Jacklin in 1969, it seems that home players have done everything but win.

The frustration is compounded because it appears that lesser golfing countries can do as well if not better. France and Argentina, neither of which is a hotbed of golf, each have one Open champion. From West Germany, where there are fewer than 100,000 golfers, comes Bernhard Langer, good enough to have come second in two of the four Opens between 1981 and 1984. No wonder the average Briton, the man arguing about sport in the pub, is saying: 'If they can do it, why can't we?'

This feeling of chauvinism arises each mid-summer and is often directed at Faldo because his record is the most consistent of domestic professionals. Since turning pro in 1976 he has survived to the end of the nine Opens up to and including 1984. His worst was not, as you might expect, in his first Open, by which time he had been a pro for only a couple of months, but in 1977, when he finished joint 62nd. Much more satisfactory have been the results in 1978, 1982, 1983 and 1984 – joint sixth, joint fourth, joint eighth and joint sixth respectively.

His scoring has been a model of consistency – an average of 71.79 for the 36 rounds. Whereas his worst rounds have been 78's at Birkdale in 1976 and Turnberry the following year, other more distinguished players have soared to higher figures. Lee Trevino and Johnny Miller have both had 79's, Tom Watson has had an 81 and Jack Nicklaus took an 83 during the Open at Royal St George's in 1981.

You have only to watch Faldo preparing for an Open to realise how seriously he regards the championship. He demonstrates as much thoroughness as Jack Nicklaus did when he first began competing in the Open in the early nineteen sixties. As he sought to learn about each Open course, Nicklaus would play in every possible wind. Sometimes he would give up after nine holes and not return until the afternoon when the capricious winds that blow over the seaside courses, on which the Open is traditionally staged, would have moved to another point of the compass. On some holes Nicklaus used to drive deliberately into the rough so that he knew what to expect and he would spend ten or fifteen minutes on the greens aiming his putts at where he anticipated the flags would be positioned during the championship.

Before the 1981 Open Faldo played five practice rounds over the rolling Kentish links. 'Nothing can be left to chance,' he said. 'You want to know the course so well you know it by heart. In the end you want to go to sleep at night thinking about it.'

It is significant for Faldo in his quest for this victory that he has been heavily influenced by events that occur in July, the month of the Open. He was born on July 18th, his mother was born on the 22nd, his girl-friend Gill on July 12th. The birthdays of John Simpson, Faldo's manager, best man and closest friend and of Tony Jacklin, his predecessor as Britain's leading golfer, also fall in July. Faldo received his first set of golf clubs in July and won the English Amateur, the most prized of his amateur victories, in July. That is not all. In July 1978 Faldo shot his lowest competitive round in Europe, a 64 in the German Open. At least it was his lowest until he had a 62 in the Lawrence Batley tournament in 1983 – in July, again, of course.

Another statistic worth mentioning is that a year after winning their first event on the US tour, Gary Player, Tony Jacklin and Seve Ballesteros went on to win their first Open.

Upon being given £100 for winning the Open, Henry Cotton said he would have paid £10,000 of his own money to have won because the event meant so much to him. Faldo has as much enthusiasm and reverence for the Open as Cotton. 'The other tournaments I have won are important and I am delighted I won them but I'd trade them in for the Open,' says Faldo. 'It's the oldest trophy in international golf and the only one of the four major championships held in Britain and on a links course. Anyone born in Britain must want to win at home. Don't get me wrong. I'd love to win the US Open or the Masters but the one I want more than any other is the Open. I feel I can win it. I know I can win it. I've been close enough now, I ought to know what it's like on that last afternoon.'

There remains one commodity necessary for Faldo to win an Open and unfortunately for him it is one that he cannot supply. He can acquaint himself with every blade of grass on the course and can have studied every one of its eighteen holes in all possible winds. He can be hitting the ball better than ever and putting like an inspired Ben Crenshaw. But all that, considerable as it is, is not enough. 'Whatever anybody thinks, to win a major championship you have not only to be playing well but you also have to have the breaks,' says Tony Jacklin, who won two of golf's major championships between July 1969 and June 1970. 'The luck doesn't have to be Nick playing good – it can be someone else falling over. Look, I know. I played better in 1968 at Carnoustie, apart from my last round, and at Muirfield in 1972, than I did when I won at Lytham. Between 1967 and 1972 I was always there or thereabouts in the Open but out of that lot I only won one. If Nick stays around long enough then the chances are that victory will come his way. But it takes time. Look at Nicklaus. He has won three Opens but come second or third maybe ten or twelve times.'

As Faldo and his contemporaries pursue the four major championships, they ought to say a silent prayer of thanks for three men without whom golf might now be little more than an idiosyncratic diversion, rather as real tennis or polo are at present. The three men in question are an Englishman, a Channel Islander and a Scotsman who together make up The Great Triumvirate. J. H. Taylor, Harry Vardon and James Braid were born within thirteen months of one another at almost precisely the mid-point of Queen Victoria's reign. From 1894 to 1914 they were to rule the world of golf far more completely than did Arnold Palmer, Jack Nicklaus and Gary Player half a century later. They won the Open sixteen times between them during this remarkable span of just over two decades. It became **their** competition and on the rare occasions when another competitor was victorious either Taylor, Vardon or Braid always finished second. At Muirfield in 1906 they did even better than that: Braid won the Open, Taylor came second and Vardon was third.

Vardon, the Channel Islander, was the most accomplished of the three, if only because his victory in the US Open of 1900 gave him a total of seven major championships. As well as giving his name to the most popular grip in golf, Vardon won his last and a record sixth Open when he was forty-four. For their parts, Braid, who was the son of an Ely ploughman and who became pro at Walton Heath Golf Club in Surrey, where he often played with the Prince of Wales, and the Devonian James Henry Taylor both won the Open on five occasions.

Almost as great an achievement as this was the way the Triumvirate spread the game throughout Britain and the US, thereby raising its standing and, by the way, its financial appeal. At a time when travelling really was travelling, and involved considerable discomfort, and perhaps actual hardship, such as modern golfers fortunately do not have to endure, Vardon, Taylor and Braid took golf to the people, playing matches in front of a public that was beginning to appreciate the charms of this new sport. Vardon, in particular, appeared to have an insatiable appetite for challenge matches, the most notable being one against Willie Park over two legs, the first at North Berwick and the second at Ganton. Prize money was the considerable sum for those days of £100 a side and the imagination of the public was so caught that 7,000 spectators turned out at North Berwick to watch.

Vardon, who was born in Grouville, Jersey, made his first tour to the US in 1900. It's hard to imagine now, what with players whizzing from one continent to the next within a few days, just how much of a missionary visit this must have been. It began in March and continued until the end of the year, except for a break in mid-summer when he returned to Britain for the Open. Later, by now back in the US, he criss-crossed the vast country from Florida to Portland, Oregon, and back to the east coast again. Thirteen years later Vardon was to make a second grand tour of the US, this time with Edward (Ted) Ray, another outstanding golfer of the Edwardian era. They travelled 30,000 miles to all four corners of the US and up to Canada as well, competed on fifty different courses and went from place to place at night. If that's not spreading the gospel then I don't know what is.

So Faldo must doff his cap to Taylor, Vardon and Braid, but to whom else? Of today's pros he is one of the nattiest dressers, favouring the brightest primary colours. When on tour in the US he carries in his luggage at least one dozen coordinated outfits made up of twelve shirts, eight pairs of trousers, cashmere sweaters, and three pairs of golf shoes. Faldo is a Beau Brummel alongside, say, Neil Coles, who rarely varies from good old grey, but he would look positively dowdy next to Walter Hagen, the pro who started the fashion for brightly-coloured clothes.

Hagen was a terrific golfer who had twice been American Open champion by the time he arrived at Southampton, in 1920, on his first visit to Britain. But he is remembered as being as great a character as he was golfer, a man who, in the words of another pro, was 'in golf to live – not to make a living'. Hagen won more than seventy-five championships and over a million dollars but is remembered most of all for saying, 'I never wanted to be a millionaire – I just wanted to live like one . . .'. The American author Herbert Warren Wind, writing in **The Story of American Golf**, said, 'Great as he was as a golfer, Hagen was even greater as a personality – an artist with a sense of timing so infallible that he could make the tying of his shoelaces more dramatic than the other guy's hole in one.'

Hagen, who was later to inspire so many fellow professionals to follow his example and dress colourfully, was himself inspired by a relatively unknown American pro named Tom Anderson. 'Tom had class!' Hagen has recalled. 'His outfit just knocked my eyes out. His shirt was pure white silk with bright red, blue, yellow and black stripes. His immaculate white flannel pants had the cuffs turned up. He wore a red bandanna knotted casually around his neck and a loud plaid cap on his head. In my small town life he was the most tremendous personality I'd ever seen. His white buckskin shoes had thick red rubber soles and sported the widest white laces any two shoes could carry. I decided right then to copy that outfit from white buckskins to bandanna.'

Accordingly he arrived in Deal for his first practice round for the 1920 Open with twelve different outfits, all colour coordinated: black sleeveless sweaters, white silk shirts with collar and dark tie, tailored white flannelled knickerbockers and black and white sports shoes. Though he looked a million dollars he played like a pauper and trailed in 53rd out of a field of 54. 'I'm sorry you didn't go better 'Aigen,' said a patronising British official who had earlier had Hagen removed from the locker room and told to change in the pro's shop. 'Golf over 'ere is very difficult. Come back and try again sometime.'

Faldo, a child of the nineteen fifties and the late nineteen fifties at that, is much too young to remember the period of extreme social prejudice in golf. In those days pros were not allowed into clubs, not even to change their shoes, for fear they might mix with the members who were all, it goes without saying, perfect gentlemen. Now the situation has changed so much, it is the members who are kicked out of their changing rooms during tournaments while the pros are lionised. Caddies, however, are still banned from clubhouses and compelled to while away their idle hours in a caddies' shack.

Hagen was one of the men who was responsible for the signal upgrading in the status of pros. When told he was unable to enter the dining room and changing rooms of clubs where he had just played, he would retire to his rented Rolls-Royce and be served a sumptuous meal by liveried footmen. He had an ally in this cause in Henry Cotton, who came along ten years later and by protests against this sort of treatment and other matters made himself unpopular with his fellow pros. For this, he was excluded from three Ryder Cup teams.

In considering the similarities and dissimilarities in character and circumstances between some of the key figures in the history of the Open, Cotton is sometimes the exception who proves the general rule. Whereas Vardon, Taylor, Braid and Hagen all came from modest backgrounds, as did Jacklin (and as does Faldo) and scarcely accumulated any academic achievements at school (and again the same can be said of Jacklin and Faldo), Cotton was a product of the middle classes, public-school educated and destined for a career appropriate to his background. But he was not lacking in that characteristic that is so important to champions, a bump of irreverence, a reluctance to conform for the sake of conformity.

Cotton's irreverence surfaced early, when after a school cricket match he refused to carry the bags of some senior boys. To make matters worse, he declined to be caned for this act of mutiny. Told that he would be .banned from cricket thereafter, Cotton as much as said 'so be it' and turned to golf. As is often the case, such a small incident affected the rest of his life. Soon after he turned sixteen Cotton left school to become a professional golfer and went on to win three Opens, the only Englishman to do this since J. H. Taylor three quarters of a century ago. For a while Cotton was one of the best golfers in the world. But for the Second World War, which interrupted his career the way the Great War had interrupted Hagen's, Cotton would surely have won more titles.

One day in the autumn of 1984, a colleague posed a question: which of Bernhard Langer, Greg Norman and Nick Faldo would be the first to win a major title? The question was intriguing. The safe bet would be Norman, the Australian who was thirty in February 1985. He had gone closest of the three by forcing a play-off with Fuzzy Zoeller in the 1984 US Open at Winged Foot. Big, strong, fearless and confident, Norman won the Kemper and Canadian Opens of 1984, two World Matchplay Championships, as well as coming fourth in the 1981 Masters. 'Greg's a big strong player. He'll probably win a green jacket one day,' said Jack Nicklaus after playing with Norman in the third round. Norman's best chance is in either the US Open or the US PGA. He hits the ball too high to be at his best on an exposed, fast running course such as those on which the Open is staged. His record in this event is poor. Only once between 1978 and 1984 did he finish in the top ten.

A gambler might go for Faldo or Langer. The German has improved by leaps and bounds since he won the European money list in 1981 and become such a good striker that Mark McCormack, his manager, said in the autumn of 1984, 'From tee to green Langer is the best in the world at the moment.' As if to make the point, Langer defeated Norman in a semi-final of the 1984 Suntory World Matchplay Championship.

Can Faldo compete with either of these two? Certainly he can, though he has never finished as high at Augusta as Norman in 1981, nor done so well in the Open as Langer, who came second in 1981 and 1984. Faldo has advantages over them both, nonetheless. He has already won a tournament on the American circuit, something that Langer had not achieved by February 1984. And there's no doubt that Faldo's consistency in the Open and the support he receives, notably when it is played in England, help him to raise his game to a level that is higher than Norman's in this venerable event. Norman has yet to finish ahead of Faldo in the Open.

Walter Hagen said years ago that golf champions are made and not born. That being so, any embryonic champion would benefit from shopping around among former champions, taking a little from each of them. It would be helpful to have some of Hagen's nerve. He used to breeze into tournaments, particularly matchplay events at which he was well nigh unbeatable, and say, 'Well, fellas, who's gonna come second?' Max Faulkner, Open champion in 1951, was fairly cool also. When he was leading at halfway in the Open at Royal Portrush, he took to signing autographs 'Max Faulkner, Open Champion 1951'. As much as possible of Arnold Palmer's charisma and Jack Nicklaus's concentration would be invaluable and so would a measure of Gary Player's determination. As a teenager with a terrible grip and a small physique, the South African would plant himself in front of a mirror and repeat out loud: 'I am going to be the greatest golfer in the world.'

From Tony Jacklin our would-be champion could take self-belief. Though Jacklin was not given the advantage of being born near a golf course or in one of the many golf-dominated corners of Britain, he never had a moment's doubt that he would make his mark in golf. He knew he would win bundles of money, buy a big car, live in a large house and generally behave as sportsmen from modest backgrounds are supposed to do when they strike it rich. And he convinced everyone else he would do these things too.

Self-belief being more than half the battle, he achieved all this and more. He forecast that he would win a tournament on the American circuit in 1968. When he duly succeeded at Jacksonville he was the only person who wasn't surprised, although no Briton had won an Open tournament in the US for fifty years. Then, in 1969, he won the Open at Lytham by two shots, but this wasn't enough. Eleven months later he smashed the rest of a very strong field in the US Open to win by an astonishing seven strokes.

When the world lay at his feet following this stunning achievement, Jacklin gave the impression that it was no more than he deserved. After all, he was, in the words of Henry Longhurst in the **Sunday Times**, 'the steam-fitter's apprentice who went seven up on the wide world of golf'. His grinning face, with teeth as regular and gleaming as a newly-painted picket fence, peered out from advertisements. He commanded £3,000 for a day's golf clinic, £2,000 in appearance money at tournaments. He was twenty-six, famous and a millionaire, just as he had predicted he would be when he was a young assistant professional earning £2.10s a week.

If we continue in our task of pilfering characteristics from champions, then from Seve Ballesteros we would take his desire to win. Hagen said, 'I always played to win, whether it was pool, marbles, baseball, shooting or golf.' The Spaniard, a man of a different era and different ethos, is the same. I watched him play his first game of pool. At first he was clumsy and slow but within an hour or so he had mastered the game sufficiently to be able to defeat those who had introduced him to the game. A story is told of Vicente Ballesteros and his younger brother Seve and it illustrates how deeply ingrained in the youngest Ballesteros is the instinct to win. Vicente was leading Seve in a competition many years ago and, seeing how downcast Seve had become at his poor play, was feeling sorry for him. Seve discovered some form and by the end of the round had overtaken Vicente and won the event. Seve was puzzled though and asked Vicente, 'Why didn't you want to win? Why did you give up?'

Tom Watson's contribution to our putative champion is expertise at dealing with the press. Watson has the respect of journalists because he is articulate, as you would expect of a psychology graduate, and he cares about the wider issues of golf. The respect in which he is held is not diminished in his case by a reluctance to talk about matters other than golf, a practice that journalists find irritating in some of Watson's contemporaries. Watson employs the old technique of col-laborating fully on golf questions, which absolves him from having to answer endless questions about himself. He has succeeded in separating golf from life. To my knowledge he has never spoken about his support for the Liberal, George McGovern, in the 1972 Presidential elections. Little is known about Watson's house in a select suburb of Kansas City, his reading habits or his taste in music, and the same journalists who normally love to ferret out this sort of information from anyone as well known as Watson leave him alone on these issues. Watson is the least-known, best-liked golfer.

Now that we have created a paragon, a man who can't possibly lose, we had better make sure he knows how to enjoy all the money that is going to materialise. This is where

Henry Cotton comes in. Dressed in cashmeres and silks, he gave lessons to the high and mighty and lived and entertained like a king. He served champagne and caviar at elegant parties at his home in Eaton Square, London, and was waited on hand and foot in his luxurious home in Penina, Portugal. He never had any difficulty in getting rid of money in style.

So much for the theoretical; what about the practice? Who are the real champions? 'In the end the real champions are those who have had the guts to go out after it for themselves,' says Jacklin. 'They get involved in the process of learning how to win and then go and do it themselves.' That is borne out by his experience, by Hagen's and Seve Ballesteros's. They, unlike Jack Nicklaus, whose father was a member of a country club with an outstanding golf course, had to find their own way to a golf club, scrape together money to buy equipment and forage for balls. Many of them began as caddies and Ballesteros had the extra disadvantage of being banned from playing on the golf course for 364 days of the year. He was able to play only in the caddies' championship. He got round this ban by sneaking out at night to the holes furthest from the clubhouse and playing by moonlight.

Amateur golf in Britain and Ireland has not been very successful at breeding champions for the professional game. Faldo is one of the very few to have gone from English Amateur Champion to becoming a realistic contender for the Open. Why is this? Are there too few junior events? In the late nineteen fifties and early sixties there existed in Gloucestershire a thriving junior section of boys from all over the county. Domestic competitions were arranged and in the Easter and summer holidays teams were raised to play in matches against Yorkshire and other counties. Some of the juniors who first came to prominence in those matches remain stalwarts of the county's senior team and thus the initiative of the Gloucestershire officials has been rewarded. By the same token the Golf Foundation's competition for schools, run in conjunction with Aer Lingus, and the **Daily Express** National Boys' Championship are also to be applauded.

But they are too little and possibly too late. The truth is that juniors are still treated poorly at many clubs. Faldo recalls sitting next to a committee member at a recent club dinner. The conversation was pleasantly non-committal until the member said he thought it was ridiculous that juniors were allowed to play on his course for £10 a year. Faldo saw red on hearing that. 'That's a very blinkered attitude,' he said. 'Your junior members of today are the committee men of tomorrow. Plus, if you don't encourage juniors, where are the Walker Cup and Ryder Cup teams going to come from? Besides, if you organise the juniors you'll find after a few years you have a regular stream of good players eligible for the club's senior teams and you'll have something to be proud of. It happened at the club where I learned to play. We had a young go-ahead captain and he got a junior section going and ever since, Welwyn has had one of the strongest groups of juniors in the county.' The attitude of the club member to whom Faldo addressed these remarks is one that suggests it will be left to the Swedes to do in golf what they have done so successfully in tennis – form and finance a junior squad that could produce some world-class players in a few years.

In the end necessity is the mother of invention and self-generated incentive is the greatest spur. I once asked Ballesteros whether he would have wanted to have learned his golf in another, less inconvenient, way? 'I didn't mind starting as I did,' he replied. 'The easier you have it the less anxious you are to fight. You lose interest. You lose the dream. How can you dream of a cup of coffee if you have it already?'

'When I was a boy the closest I ever lived to a course was four miles away and I cycled there and back every day for years,' says Tony Jacklin. 'My children live on a golf course, get free practice balls, have new clubs and one of Europe's best courses on which to play. As a result they are only half interested. You have to want it, have to fight for it. Most of the young guys who have made it in the UK, including TJ, have made it on their own. It hasn't changed a lot in twenty years and I don't think it will change much in the next twenty.'

What chance is there that Faldo can become Open champion, only the eleventh from Britain or Ireland since 1914? It's a daunting task and the odds are even longer than they might seem. Nowadays the Open always attracts a good many Americans in addition to many of the leading golfers from other parts of the world, whereas of the ten victories since 1914 only Duncan's (1920), Havers's (1923), Cotton's in 1937 and Jacklin's were from truly international fields. Few Americans entered in 1935, 1936, 1938, 1939, 1947 and 1951 when Alf Perry, Alf Padgham, Reg Whitcombe, Dick Burton, Fred Daly and Max Faulkner were successful.

Even against these odds there is no shortage of supporters to speak on Faldo's behalf. The first was Johnny Miller, who forecast some years ago that Faldo would win the Open. Gary Player has likened Faldo to one of a number of outstanding racehorses, any one of which could burst clear in the last furlong of the big race. 'Nick has the mental capacity and capability to win the Open,' says Tony Jacklin, a view endorsed by Jacklin's predecessor as Ryder Cup captain, John Jacobs. Though it hardly needs me to add anything I will make a prediction nonetheless. I am sure that Faldo will win the Open before he reaches his 31st birthday.

Epilogue

One afternoon in March Nick Faldo and I sat side by side on a sofa in IMG's London office, and went through the manuscript of this book line by line. It was less fun than a round of golf with Faldo would have been. There were moments when I felt that a five-minute argument over my use of the words 'next to' rather than 'with' was allowing my subject to collaborate too closely. But then I remembered what I had written again and again in the preceding pages – in matters to do with golf, Faldo is a perfectionist. Later, when I thought back to our five-hour reading session, I came to admire Faldo's professionalism in wanting to make sure that everything was just so.

Faldo gets involved in controversies as often as a child walks through puddles. Often these controversies are no more than misunderstandings that have been blown out of proportion by both sides. The 'El Foldo' incident is a perfect example of one such. The nickname that he was allegedly given by some of the British press after the 1984 Masters created bad feelings between Faldo and the British press, who have not always been on the best of terms. It was later found to be a complete misunderstanding. No paper had carried a headline or story using that phrase. Just as unfortunate was the letter sent to **Golf World** by an angry Irishman complaining about Faldo's discourteous behaviour in the 1984 Irish Open pro-am. This correspondent was later discredited but, by then, the damage to Faldo's reputation had been done.

I have spent more time in Faldo's company than any other

journalist and the man I have seen across the dinner table in Europe and the US is not the taciturn Faldo of public image. He is an engaging dinner companion, a good mimic and story-teller, and, as he matures, able to talk about rather more than just his passions of pop music and fast cars. A most gifted golfer is Nicholas Alexander Faldo; a most misunderstood one as well.

Appendix

Faldo's final amateur year, 1975

Royston Junior Boys' Championship, Royston GC, Cambs., April 3. Faldo (Welwyn Garden City GC) 73, 67 – 140. 1st.

Hertfordshire Junior County Championship, Verulam GC, St Albans, April 15. Faldo 72, 72 – 144. 1st.

English Open Amateur Stroke Play Championship for the Brabazon Trophy, Notts GC, Hollinwell, May 16–18. Faldo 76, 75, 74, 81 – 306. Jt 7th.

The Berkshire Trophy, The Berkshire GC. Ascot, June 14–15. Faldo 71, 70, 68, 72 – 281. 1st. (Aged 17, Faldo was the youngest winner of the Berkshire Trophy.)

The Scrutton Jug awarded to the player with the lowest aggregate in the Brabazon and the Berkshire. Faldo 306, 281 – 587. 1st.

Hertfordshire County Championship, Ashridge GC, Little Gaddesden, June 22-25. Faldo def. R. A. Durrant (Moor Park) 5 & 4. (Faldo now holds both the senior and junior county championship titles of Hertfordshire.)

The King George V Coronation Challenge Cup, Porters Park GC, Radlett, June 28. Faldo tied with C. Phillips (Dulwich & Sydenham GC) on 146. Phillips def. Faldo at 4th hole of play-off.

The English Amateur Championship, Royal Lytham and St Anne's GC, July 21–26. Fifth rd: Faldo def. B. J. Winteridge 2 holes; sixth rd: Faldo def. G. M. Edwards 2 & 1; semi-final: Faldo def. P. Morley 4 & 3. Final: Faldo def. D. J. Eccleston 6 & 4. (Eight days past his 18th birthday, Faldo is the youngest-ever English Amateur champion.)

England v Scotland, Youths' International, Pannal GC, Harrogate, August 5. Foursomes: Faldo, J. A. Watts (East Herts.) lost to I. Gillan (Bishoprigg), R. G. Cairns (Lundin Links) 1 hole. Singles: Faldo def. S. Stephen (Lundin Links) 4 & 3.

Great Britain & Ireland v Continent of Europe, Youths' International, Pannal, August 6. Foursomes: Faldo, Stephen def. A. Lionello, M. Manelli (Italy) 1 hole. Singles: Faldo def. Manelli 2 & 1.

British Youths' Championship, Pannal, August 7–9. Faldo 65, 74, 70, 69 – 278. 1st.

Home Internationals, Portmarnock GC, Dublin, September 10–12. England v Scotland: Foursomes, G. C. Marks, Faldo halved with G. MacGregor, A. K. Pirie. Singles, Faldo lost to D. G. Greig 1 hole.
England v Wales: Foursomes, Faldo, Marks def. M. P. D. Adams, I. Duffy 1 hole. Singles, Faldo def. J. G. Jermine 7 & 5.
England v Ireland: Foursomes, Faldo, Marks def. H. B. Smyth, J. Harrington 5 & 4. Singles, Faldo def. M. D. O'Brien 1 hole.
Faldo scored 4½ points out of six.

Welwyn Garden City Golf Club, club championship, final, September 21. Faldo def. D. C. Allen 7 & 5.

County Champions' Tournament for the President's Bowl, Kedleston Park GC, Kedleston, Derbys. September 28. Faldo 70, 70 – 140. 1st.

South African Golf Union Special Stroke Play Championship, Mowbray GC, Cape Town, November 11–13. Faldo – 298 defeated Stuart Jones (New Zealand) and Gerald Williams (Western Province) at fifth hole of play-off.

British Commonwealth Trophy Tournament, Royal Durban GC, November 18–22. GB def. New Zealand 5–4, South Africa 5–4, lost to Canada 3–6. Faldo in Great Britain team.

Faldo's results in The Open, 1976–1984

1976
Royal Birkdale, Southport, England, July 7–10. Par 72. Winner: Johnny Miller (US) 72, 68, 73, 66 – 279. Faldo: 78, 71, 76, 69 – 294. Jt 28th with Gary Player (S. Africa), Neil Coles (England), Doug Sanders (US). Prize money: £335.

1977
Turnberry, Scotland, July 6–9. Par 70. Winner: Tom Watson (US) 68, 70, 65, 65 – 268. Faldo 71, 76, 74, 78 – 299. Jt 62nd with Vin Baker (S. Africa), Silvano Locatelli (Italy). Prize money: £250.

1978
St Andrews, Scotland, July 12–15. Par 72. Winner: Jack Nicklaus (US) 71, 72, 69, 69 – 281. Faldo 71, 72, 70, 72 – 285. Jt 10th with Isao Aoki (Japan), Bob Shearer (Australia), John Schroeder (US). Prize money: £3,937.50.

1979
Royal Lytham & St Anne's, Blackpool, England, July 18–21. Par 72. Winner: Seve Ballesteros (Spain) 73, 65, 75, 70 – 283. Faldo 74, 74, 78, 69 – 295. Jt 19th with Sandy Lyle (Scotland), Orville Moody (US), Ken Brown (Scotland), Gary Player (S. Africa). Prize money: £1,810.

1980
Muirfield, Gullane, Scotland, July 17–20. Par 71. Winner: Tom Watson (US) 68, 70, 64, 69 – 271. Faldo 69, 74, 71, 70 – 284. Jt 12th with Larry Nelson (US), Sandy Lyle (Scotland), Isao Aoki (Japan). Prize money: £4,250.

1981
Royal St George's, Sandwich, England, July 16–19. Par 70. Winner: Bill Rogers (US) 72, 66, 67, 71 – 276. Faldo 77, 68, 69, 73 – 287. Jt 11th with Lee Trevino (US), Isao Aoki (Japan). Prize money: £5,000.

1982
Royal Troon, Scotland, July 15–18. Par 72. Winner: Tom Watson (US) 69, 71, 74, 70 – 284. Faldo 73, 73, 71, 69 – 286. Jt 4th with Des Smyth (Ireland), Tom Purtzer (US), Masahiro Kuramoto (Japan). Prize money: £11,000.

1983
Royal Birkdale, Southport, England, July 14–17. Par 71. Winner: Tom Watson (US) 67, 68, 70, 70 – 275. Faldo 68, 68, 71, 73 – 280. Jt 8th with Denis Durnian (England), Christy O'Connor Jnr. (Ireland), Bill Rogers (US). Prize money: £9,625.

1984
St Andrews, Scotland, July 19–22. Par 72. Winner: Seve Ballesteros (Spain) 69, 68, 70, 69 – 276. Faldo 69, 68, 76, 69 – 282. Jt 6th with Greg Norman (Australia). Prize money: £16,390.

Results in Europe

1976
French Open, Le Touquet GC. Winner: Vincent Tshabalala 69, 70, 66, 67 – 272. Faldo 71, 72, 72, 72 – 287. Jt 38th. (The £130.83 Faldo won was his first prize money as a pro.)

Piccadilly Medal, Coventry GC, Finham Park. Winner: Sam Torrance 67, 72, 66, 72 – 277. Faldo – 302. 77th.

Penfold PGA Championship, Royal St George's, Sandwich. Winner: Neil Coles 70, 69, 71, 70 – 280, defeating Gary Player on first hole of play-off, Eamonn Darcy on third hole. Faldo – 222. Jt 56th.

Cacherel World Under 25's Championship, Royal Golf Club D'Evian, France. Winner: Eamonn Darcy 69, 68, 72, 65 – 274. Faldo 75, 71, 74, 73 – 293. 33rd.

Martini International, Ashburnham GC, Pembrey, Wales. Winner: Sam Torrance: 69, 67, 71, 73 – 280. Faldo 70, 81, 69, 83 – 303. 51st.

Greater Manchester Open, Wilmslow GC. Winner: John O'Leary 64, 68, 70, 74 – 276. Faldo 69, 72, 73, 73 – 287. Jt 26th.

Uniroyal International Championship, Moor Park GC, Rickmansworth. Winner: Tommy Horton 69, 72, 67, 69 – 277. Faldo 73, 69, 71, 75 – 288. Jt 24th.

Scandinavian Enterprises Open, Drottningholm GC, Stockholm. Winner: Hugh Baiocchi 68, 65, 70, 68 – 271. Faldo 74, 70, 71, 73 – 288. Jt 46th.

Swiss Open, Crans-sur-Sierre, Switzerland. Winner: Manuel Pinero 69, 67, 70, 68 – 274. Faldo 71, 71, 71, 73 – 286. Jt 14th.

Dutch Open, Kennemer GC, Zandvoort, The Netherlands. Winner: Seve Ballesteros 65, 73, 68, 69 – 275. Faldo 225. Jt 76th.

German Open, Frankfurt GC. Winner: Simon Hobday 67, 68, 65, 66 – 266. Faldo 71, 69, 71, 68 – 279. Jt 10th.

Carrolls Irish Open, Portmarnock GC, Dublin. Winner: Ben Crenshaw 73, 69, 69, 73 – 284. Faldo 156, missed the cut. Jt 103rd.

Sun Alliance Match Play Championship, Kings Norton GC, Birmingham. Winner: Brian Barnes def. Craig DeFoy 4 & 3. Faldo – 76, failed to pre-qualify.

Benson & Hedges International, Fulford GC, York. Winner: Graham Marsh 67, 66, 71, 68 – 272. Faldo 76, failed to pre-qualify.

Italian Open, Is Molas GC, Pula, Sardinia. Winner: Baldovino Dassu 71, 71, 69, 69 – 280. Faldo 78, 74, 76, 80 – 308. Jt 44th.

Order of Merit: 58th   Prize money: £2,112.

1977
Portuguese Open, Penina GC, Algarve. Winner: Manuel Ramos 70, 74, 75, 68 – 287. Faldo 157, missed the cut. Jt 91st.

Spanish Open, La Manga Campo de Golf, La Manga. Winner: Bernard Gallacher 70, 68, 70, 69 – 277. Faldo 70, 76, 72, 72 – 290. Jt 29th.

Madrid Open, Hipica Espanola Club de Campo, Madrid. Winner: Antonio Garrido 71, 68, 68, 71 – 278. Faldo 70, 72, 73, 69 – 284. Jt 3rd.

French Open, Le Touquet GC. Winner: Seve Ballesteros 69, 70, 71, 72 – 282. Faldo 305. Jt 68th.

Benson & Hedges International, Fulford GC, York. Winner: Antonio Garrido 72, 68, 72, 68 – 280. Faldo 297. Jt 54th.

Sun Alliance Match Play Championship, Stoke Poges GC, Slough. Winner: Hugh Baiocchi def. Brian Huggett 6 & 5. Faldo def. D Ingram 1 hole, T. Britz at 19th, L. Platts 1 hole, lost to Huggett 3 & 2.

Penfold PGA Championship, Royal St George's, Sandwich. Winner: Manuel Pinero 73, 70, 74, 66 – 283. Faldo 77, 71, 72, 69 – 288. Jt 6th.

Kerrygold Classic, Waterville GC, Co. Kerry. Winner: Liam Higgins 65, 73, 74, 75 – 287. Faldo 75, 78, 81, 86 – 320. 45th.

Greater Manchester Open, Wilmslow GC. Winner: Eamonn Darcy 69, 67, 66, 67 – 269. Faldo 149, missed the cut. Jt 94th.

Uniroyal International Championship, Moor Park GC, Rickmansworth. Winner: Seve Ballesteros 70, 70, 67, 69 – 276, defeated Faldo 68, 67, 73, 68 on first extra hole.

Swiss Open, Crans-sur-Sierre, Switzerland. Winner: Seve Ballesteros 68, 66, 70, 69 – 273. Faldo 291. Jt 53rd.

Scandinavian Enterprises Open, Drottningholms GC, Stockholm. Winner: Bob Byman 70, 69, 68, 68 – 275. Faldo 292. Jt 62nd.

Callers of Newcastle Open, Whitley Bay GC. Winner: John Fourie 66, 71, 74, 71 – 282, defeated Tommy Horton and Peter Butler on first extra hole, Angel Gallardo on second extra hole. Faldo 68, 72, 76, 73 – 289. Jt 27th.

German Open, Dusseldorf Land and Golf Club. Winner: Tienie Britz 66, 67, 71, 71 – 275. Faldo 70, 72, 68, 68 – 278. Jt 3rd.

Skol Lager Individual, Gleneagles Hotel, King's Course, Perthshire. Faldo 68, 71 – 139 defeated Craig Defoy 72, 67 and Chris Witcher 70, 69 on first extra hole. (Faldo's first victory as a pro.)

Double Diamond Classic, Gleneagles Hotel, King's Course, Perthshire. Winners: US 3½ def. Australasia ½. England def. 3–1 in first rd. Ian Stanley def. Faldo 3 & 2. England halved with Rest of World 2–2, Faldo lost to Kazuo Yoshikawa 2 & 1.

Carrolls Irish Open, Portmarnock GC, Dublin. Winner: Hubert Green 70, 69, 74, 70 – 283. Faldo 73, 72, 71, 73 – 289. Jt 9th.

Laurent Perrier Trophy, Royal Waterloo GC, Brussels. Faldo 69, 69, 70 – 208. 1st.

Dunlop Masters, Lindrick GC, Worksop. Winner: Guy Hunt 74, 70, 76, 71 – 291 defeated Brian Barnes 68, 78, 72, 73 on third extra hole. Faldo 83 withdrew.

Colgate World Match Play Championship, The Wentworth Club, Virginia Water. Winner: G. Marsh defeated R. Floyd 5 & 3. Faldo defeated by Seve Ballesteros 4 & 2 in first rd.

Ryder Cup, Royal Lytham and St Anne's, Blackpool. Great Britain and Ireland 7½, US 12½. First day: Peter Oosterhuis, Faldo def. Lou Graham, Ray Floyd 2 & 1 (foursomes). Second day: Oosterhuis, Faldo def. J. Nicklaus, Floyd 2 & 1 (fourball). Third day: Faldo def. Watson 1 hole. Faldo won three points out of three.

Order of Merit: 8th   Prize money: £23,977.

1978

Portuguese Open, Penina GC, Algarve. Winner: Howard Clark 71, 75, 71, 74 – 291. Faldo 77, 76, 74, 75 – 302. Jt 34th.

Spanish Open, Real Club de Golf, El Prat, Barcelona. Winner: Brian Barnes 67, 75, 70, 64 – 276. Faldo 74, 72, 71, 74 – 291. Jt 40th.

Madrid Open, Real Club de la Puerta de Hierro, Madrid. Winner: Howard Clark 70, 70, 72, 70 – 282. Faldo 76, 73, 75, 74 – 298. Jt 33rd.

French Open Championship, La Baule GC, Nantes. Winner: Dale Hayes 66, 69, 67, 67 – 269. Faldo 71, 75, 73, 69 – 288. Jt 11th.

Martini International, RAC Golf and Country Club, Epsom. Winner: Seve Ballesteros 67, 67, 67, 69 – 270. Faldo 67, 70, 71, 67 – 275. 2nd.

Colgate PGA Championship, Royal Birkdale, Southport. Winner: Faldo 71, 68, 70, 69 – 278.

Belgian Open Championship, Royal Golf Club of Belgium, Brussels. Winner: Noel Ratcliffe 72, 70, 72, 66 – 280. Faldo 71, 71, 71, 72 – 285. Jt 6th.

Greater Manchester Open, Wilmslow GC. Winner: Brian Barnes 69, 71, 69, 66 – 275. Faldo – 295. Jt 73rd.

Sun Alliance Match Play Championship, Dalmahoy G and CC, Edinburgh. Winner: Mark James def. Neil Coles 3 & 2. Faldo def. Peter Berry 6 & 5 (1st rd); defeated by Gary Cullen 2 & 1 (2nd rd).

German Open Championship, Cologne-Refrath GC, Cologne. Winner: Seve Ballesteros 64, 67, 70, 67 – 268. Faldo 64, 73, 70, 71 – 278. 11th.

Scandinavian Enterprises Open, Vasatorps GC, Helsingborg. Winner: Seve Ballesteros 73, 69, 68, 69 – 279. Faldo 75, 77, 67, 69 – 288. Jt 16th.

Benson & Hedges International, Fulford GC, York. Winner: Lee Trevino 69, 67, 72, 66 – 274 defeated Noel Ratcliffe on first extra hole, Coles on fourth. Faldo 70, 68, 66, 71 – 275. Jt 4th.

Carrolls Irish Open, Portmarnock GC, Dublin. Winner: Ken Brown 70, 71, 70, 70 – 281. Faldo 73, 73, 74, 69 – 289. Jt 18th.

Swiss Open, Crans-sur-Sierre. Winner: Seve Ballesteros 68, 68, 68, 68 – Faldo 68, 68, 72, 76 – 284. Jt 18th.

Laurent Perrier Trophy, Royal Waterloo GC, Brussels. Winner: Faldo 69, 72, 68 – 209 defeated Seve Ballesteros 67, 72, 70, on second hole of play-off.

Tournament Players' Championship, Foxhills G and CC, Chertsey. Winner: Brian Waites 75, 69, 73, 69 – 286. Faldo 305. Jt 52nd.

Hennessy Cognac Cup, The Belfry, Sutton Coldfield. Winners: Gt Britain and Ireland 17½ pts, Europe 14½. Faldo lost two singles, one foursome with John O'Leary and won one fourball with O'Leary.

Dunlop Masters, St Pierre G and CC, Chepstow. Winner: T. Horton 71, 70, 67, 71 – 279. Faldo 70, 75, 72, 75 – 292. Jt 24th.

Colgate World Match Play Championship, The Wentworth Club, Virginia Water. Winner: Isao Aoki def. Simon Owen 3 & 2. Faldo def. Andy Bean 5 & 4, was def. by Graham Marsh by 1 hole.

European Open, Walton Heath GC, Tadworth, Surrey. Winner: Bobby Wadkins 71, 72, 72, 68 – 283, defeated Bernard Gallacher and Gil Morgan on first extra hole. Faldo 68, 70, 75, 71 – 284. Jt 4th.

Order of Merit: 3rd   Prize money: £37,911.

1979

Italian Open Championship, Monticello GC, Como. Winner: Brian Barnes 73, 70, 71, 67 – 281 defeated Dale Hayes on fourth hole of sudden death. Faldo 73, 76, 75, 73 – 297. Jt 44th.

French Open Championship, Lyon GC, Lyon. Winner: Bernard Gallacher 71, 69, 74, 70 – 284. Faldo 72, 72, 73, 71 – 288. Jt 5th.

Colgate PGA Championship, Old Course, St Andrews. Winner: Vicente Fernandez 71, 70, 72, 75 – 281. Faldo 65, 70, 78, 79 – 292. Jt 10th.

Martini International, The Wentworth Club, Virginia Water. Winner: Greg Norman 75, 67, 72, 74 – 288. Faldo 151, missed cut. Jt 52nd.

Belgian Open Championship, Royal Waterloo GC, Brussels. Winner: Gavin Levenson 68, 71, 68, 72 – 279. Faldo 69, 72, 70, 71 – 282. Jt 2nd.

The Welsh Classic, Wenvoe Castle GC, Cardiff. Winner: Mark James 72, 68, 68, 70 – 278 defeated Eddie Polland, Mike Miller on third hole of sudden death. Faldo 74, 70, 73, 65 – 282. 10th.

Lada English Golf Classic, The Belfry, Sutton Coldfield. Winner: Seve Ballesteros 73, 71, 71, 71 – 286. Faldo 72, 71, 77, 73 – 293. Jt 4th.

Scandinavian Enterprises Open, Vasatorps GC, Helsingborg. Winner: Sandy Lyle 73, 69, 65, 69 – 276. Faldo 69, 78, 74, 71 – 292. Jt 20th.

Sun Alliance Match Play Championship, Fulford GC, York. Winner: Des Smyth defeated Nick Price 1 hole. Faldo defeated in first round by Mike Steadman 1 hole.

Benson & Hedges International, St Mellion G and CC, St Mellion, Plymouth. Winner: Maurice Bembridge 67, 67, 69, 69 – 272. Faldo 75, 71, 68, 66 – 280. Jt 12th.

German Open, Frankfurt GC, Frankfurt. Winner: Tony Jacklin 68, 68, 70, 71 – 277. Faldo 72, 75, 73, 71 – 291. Jt 30th.

Carrolls Irish Open, Portmarnock, Dublin. Winner: Mark James 73, 75, 69, 65 – 282. Faldo 78, 71, 69, 75 – 293. Jt 26th.

Swiss Open Championship, Crans-sur-Sierre. Winner: Hugh Baiocchi 68, 67, 73, 67 – 275. Faldo 156, missed the cut. Jt 117th.

European Open, Turnberry Hotel, Ayrshire. Winner: Sandy Lyle 71, 67, 72, 65 – 275. Faldo 73, 74, 70, 75 – 292. Jt 29th.

Sun Alliance Ryder Cup, Greenbrier GC, West Virginia. US 17 pts, Europe 11. First day: P. Oosterhuis, Faldo lost to A. Bean, L. Elder 2 & 1 (fourballs). Second day: Faldo, Oosterhuis def. Bean, T. Kite 6 & 5 (foursomes); Faldo, Oosterhuis def. Elder, M. Hayes 1 hole (fourballs). Third day: Faldo def. Elder 3 & 2. Faldo won three points out of four.

S.O.S. Talisman Tournament Players' Championship, Moor Park, Rickmansworth. Winner: Michael King 71, 67, 72, 71 – 281. Faldo 72, 72, 78, 72 – 294. 23rd.

Cacharel Under-25 Championship, Golf Club de Nimes, France. Winner: Bernhard Langer 73, 67, 67, 67 – 274. Faldo 73, 79, 75, 75 – 300. Jt 9th.

Dunlop Masters, Woburn G and CC. Winner: Graham Marsh 70, 68, 72, 73 – 283. Faldo 71, 76, 75, 72 – 294. Jt 19th.

Order of Merit: 21st   Prize money: £14,910.

1980

Italian Open Championship, Rome Golf Club, Acquasanta. Winner: Massimo Mannelli 68, 66, 70, 72 – 276. Faldo 73, 67, 69, 73 – 282. Jt 4th.

Madrid Open, Real Club de la Puerta de Hierro, Madrid. Winner: Seve Ballesteros 68, 63, 70, 69 – 270. Faldo 72, 74, 72, 72 – 290. Jt 18th.

Benson & Hedges Spanish Open, Escorpion Golf Club, Valencia. Winner: Eddie Polland 70, 69, 68, 69 – 276. Faldo 69, 72, 71, 73 – 285. Jt 8th.

Martini International, The Wentworth Club, Virginia Water. Winner: Seve Ballesteros 74, 75, 67, 70 – 286. Faldo 72, 78, 75, 79 – 304. Jt 36th.

Sun Alliance PGA Championship, Royal St George's, Sandwich. Winner: Faldo 73, 70, 71, 69 – 283.

Avis-Jersey Open, La Moye GC. Winner: Jose-Maria Canizares 71, 67, 71, 72 – 281. Faldo 74, 67, 75, 70 – 286. Jt 4th.

Newcastle Brown '900' Open, The Northumberland GC. Winner: Des Smyth 67, 70, 70, 69 – 276. Faldo 71, 71, 74, 73 – 289. Jt 41st.

Cold Shield Greater Manchester Open, Wilmslow GC. Winner: Des Smyth 67, 71, 69, 66 – 273 defeated Brian Waites 69, 69, 67, 68 on sixth extra hole. Faldo 67, 72, 70, 67 – 276. Jt 6th.

Coral Welsh Classic, Royal Porthcawl GC. Winner: Sandy Lyle 72, 69, 67, 69 – 277. Faldo 71, 71, 74, 70 – 286. Jt 4th.

Mazda Cars English Classic, The Belfry, Sutton Coldfield. Winner: Manuel Pinero 69, 69, 72, 76 – 286. Faldo 71, 75, 77, 77 – 300. Jt 29th.

Benson & Hedges International Open, Fulford GC, York. Winner: Graham Marsh 65, 64, 73, 70 – 272. Faldo 74, 72, 68, 67 – 281. Jt 18th.

Carrolls Irish Open, Portmarnock GC, Dublin. Winner: Mark James 71, 66, 74, 73 – 284. Faldo 72, 75, 72, 76 – 295. Jt 36th.

Braun German Open, Berlin G and CC, Wannsee. Winner: Mark McNulty 71, 70, 70, 69 – 280. Faldo 73, 75, 67, 73 – 288. Jt 12th.

European Open Championship, Walton Heath GC, Tadworth. Winner: Tom Kite 71, 67, 71, 75 – 284. Faldo – 150, missed the cut. Jt 80th.

Hennessy Cognac Cup, Sunningdale, Berkshire. Winner: Gt. Britain/ Ireland 16½, Europe 13½. Faldo won one foursome, one fourball, one single, halved one single and lost one single.

Haig Whisky Tournament Players' Championship, Moortown GC, Leeds. Winner: Bernard Gallacher 68, 65, 66, 69 – 268. Faldo 69, 68, 67, 67 – 271. Jt 2nd.

Bob Hope British Classic, RAC Golf and Country Club, Epsom. Winner: Jose-Maria Canizares 68, 67, 70, 64 – 269. Faldo 66, 70, 67, 74 – 277. Jt 17th.

Dunlop Masters, St Pierre G and CC, Chepstow. Winner: Bernhard Langer 70, 65, 67, 68 – 270. Faldo 71, 68, 71, 68 – 278. 3rd.

Suntory World Match Play Championship, The Wentworth Club, Virginia Water. Winner: Greg Norman def. Sandy Lyle 1 hole. First rd: Faldo def. David Graham 7 & 6; quarter final: Norman def. Faldo at 38th.

Lancome Trophy, St Nom-la-Breteche, Paris. Winner: Lee Trevino 68, 72, 71, 69 – 280. Faldo 75, 72, 71, 74 – 292. Jt 9th.

Order of Merit: 4th   Prize money: £46,054.

1981

Martini International, The Wentworth Club, Virginia Water. Winner: Greg Norman 71, 72, 72, 72 – 287. Faldo 73, 75, 72, 75 – 295. Jt 14th.

Sun Alliance PGA Championship, Ganton GC, N. Yorkshire. Winner: Faldo 68, 70, 67, 69 – 274.

Dunlop Masters, Woburn G and CC, Bedfordshire. Winner: Greg Norman 72, 68, 66, 67 – 273. Faldo 72, 71, 69, 70 – 282. Jt 6th.

Lawrence Batley International, Bingley St. Ives, Bradford. Winner: Sandy Lyle 70, 70, 69, 71 – 280. Faldo 71, 73, 72, 66 – 282. 2nd.

Cold Shield Greater Manchester Open, Wilmslow GC. Winner: Bernard Gallacher 65, 69, 63, 67 – 264. Faldo 67, 69, 67, 66 – 269.

Coral Classic, Royal Porthcawl, Mid-Glamorgan. Winner: Des Smyth 67, 72, 70, 73 – 282. Faldo 153, missed the cut. Jt 71st.

Scandinavian Enterprises Open, Linkoping GC, Sweden. Winner: Seve Ballesteros 69, 70, 68, 66 – 273. Faldo 72, 71, 68, 70 – 281. 3rd.

German Open, Hamburger Golf Club, Falkenstein. Winner: Bernhard Langer 67, 69, 64, 72 – 272. Faldo 72, 69, 68, 74 – 283. Jt 21st.

Carrolls Irish Open, Royal Dublin. Winner: Sam Torrance 68, 67, 69, 72 – 276. Faldo 68, 70, 71, 72 – 282. 2nd.

Benson & Hedges International Open, Fulford GC, York. Winner: Tom Weiskopf 66, 69, 68, 69 – 272. Faldo 74, 71, 73, 67 – 285. Jt 29th.

Dixcel Tissues European Open, Royal Liverpool, Hoylake. Winner: Graham Marsh 67, 72, 68, 68 – 275. Faldo 71, 74, 69, 71 – 285. Jt 14th.

Haig Whisky Tournament Players' Championship, Dalmahoy G&CC,

Edinburgh. Winner: Brian Barnes 73, 70, 71, 62 – 276 defeated Brian Waites 68, 71, 69, 68 on fourth extra hole. Faldo 71, 70, 72, 72 – 285. 29th.

Sun Alliance Ryder Cup, Walton Heath GC, Tadworth. Europe 9½, US 18½. First day: P. Oosterhuis, Faldo lost to T. Watson, J. Nicklaus 4 & 3 (foursomes). Second day: Faldo, S. Torrance lost to L. Trevino, J. Pate 7 & 5 (fourballs). Third day: Faldo def. J. Miller 2 & 1. Faldo won one point out of three.

Bob Hope British Classic, Moor Park GC, Rickmansworth. Winner: Bernhard Langer 67, 65, 68 – 200. Faldo 68, 69, 74 – 211. Jt 22nd. Rain stopped play.

Benson & Hedges Spanish Open, Real Club de Golf, El Prat, Barcelona. Winner: Seve Ballesteros 71, 67, 70, 65 – 273. Faldo 71, 71, 76, 66 – 284. Jt 20th.

Suntory World Match Play Championship, The Wentworth Club, Virginia Water. Winner: Seve Ballesteros def. Ben Crenshaw 1 hole. First rd: Crenshaw def. Faldo 5 & 3.

Lancome Trophy, St Nom-la-Breteche, Paris. Winner: David Graham 71, 72, 67, 70 – 280. Faldo 77, 70, 68, 71 – 286. 4th.

Order of Merit: 2nd   Prize money: £55,106.

1982

Martini International, Lindrick GC, Yorkshire. Winner: Bernard Gallacher 71, 71, 68, 67 – 277. Faldo 69, 74, 68, 69 – 280. Jt 2nd.

Car Care Plan International, Moor Allerton GC, Leeds. Winner: Brian Waites 68, 69, 66, 73 – 276. Faldo 72, 70, 72, 66 – 280. Jt 6th.

Sun Alliance PGA, Hillside GC, Southport. Winner: Tony Jacklin 72, 69, 73, 70 – 284. Tied with Bernhard Langer 69, 70, 73, 72. Jacklin defeated Langer on first hole of play-off. Faldo 73, 73, 73, 72 – 291. Jt 11th.

Dunlop Masters, St Pierre G and CC, Chepstow. Winner: Greg Norman 68, 69, 65, 65 – 267. Faldo 72, 68, 68, 69 – 277. Jt 7th.

Coral Classic, Royal Porthcawl, Glamorgan. Winner: Gordon Brand Jnr 69, 70, 66, 68 – 273. Faldo 70, 75, 66, 71 – 282. 7th.

State Express Classic, The Belfry, Sutton Coldfield. Winner: Greg Norman 70, 70, 70, 69 – 279. Faldo 77, 76 – 153, missed the cut.

Lawrence Batley International, Bingley St. Ives, Bradford. Winner: Sandy Lyle 70, 66, 67, 66 – 269. Faldo 68, 71, 64, 71 – 274. Jt 4th.

Carrolls Irish Open, Portmarnock GC, Dublin. Winner: John O'Leary 74, 68, 72, 73 – 287. Faldo 78, 70, 73, 69 – 290. Jt 3rd.

Benson & Hedges International Open, Fulford GC, York. Winner: Greg Norman 69, 74, 69, 71 – 283. Faldo 70, 72, 71, 72 – 285. Jt 5th.

European Open, Sunningdale, Berkshire. Winner: Manuel Pinero 68, 68, 67, 63 – 266. Faldo 70, 72, 67, 68 – 277. Jt 9th.

Hennessy Cognac Cup, Ferndown, Dorset. Gt Britain and Ireland – 106; Rest of the World – 86. Continent of Europe – 67. Indiv. prize: Mark James 64, 66, 69, 64 – 263. Faldo 67, 65, 66, 67 – 265. Jt 2nd.

Haig Whisky Tournament Players' Championship, Notts GC, Hollinwell. Faldo 69, 67, 65, 69 – 270. 1st.

Bob Hope British Classic, Moor Park GC, Rickmansworth. Winner: Gordon Brand Jnr 65, 73, 65, 68 – 272. Faldo 70, 72, 75, 69 – 286. Jt 21st.

Sanyo Open, Santu Cugat, Barcelona. Winner: Neil Coles 71, 67, 64, 64 – 266. Faldo 69, 72, 69, 67 – 277. Jt 19th.

Suntory World Matchplay Championship, The Wentworth Club, Virginia Water. Winner: Seve Ballesteros def. Sandy Lyle one up after 37 holes. First rd: Lyle def. Faldo 2 & 1.

Lancome Trophy, St Nom-la-Breteche, Paris. Winner: David Graham 66, 70, 70, 70 – 276. Faldo 70, 71, 71, 75 – 287. Jt 9th.

Portuguese Open, Penina GC, Algarve. Winner: Sam Torrance 71, 67, 69 – 207 (rain stopped play). Faldo 70, 69, 72 – 211. 2nd.

Order of Merit: 4th   Prize money: £68,252.

1983
Paco Rabanne French Open, Racing Club de France, Paris. Faldo 69, 67, 72, 69 – 277. Tied with Jose-Maria Canizares 72, 68, 70, 67 and David J. Russell 71, 72, 65, 69. Faldo defeated Russell on first extra hole, Canizares on third extra hole of play-off.

Martini International, Wilmslow GC, Cheshire. Faldo 67, 69, 66, 66 – 268. Tied with Jose-Maria Canizares 64, 70, 66, 68. Faldo defeated Canizares on third extra hole of play-off.

Car Care Plan International, Sand Moor, Leeds. Faldo 67, 68, 68, 69 – 272. 1st.

Sun Alliance PGA, Royal St George's, Sandwich. Winner: Seve Ballesteros 69, 71, 67, 71 – 278. Faldo 72, 69, 74, 75 – 290. Jt 23rd.

Silk Cut Masters, St Pierre G and CC, Chepstow. Winner: Ian Woosnam 68, 69, 67, 65 – 269. Faldo 69, 67, 69, 68 – 273. 3rd.

Times Open, Biarritz, France. Winner: Manuel Ballesteros 67, 65, 66, 64 – 262. Faldo 65, 65, 67, 67 – 264. 2nd.

Glasgow Classic, Haggs Castle GC, Glasgow. Winner: Bernhard Langer 70, 66, 66, 72 – 274. Faldo 72, 69, 67, 71 – 279. Jt 3rd.

Scandinavian Enterprises Open, Sven Tumba G and CC, Ullna, Sweden. Winner: Sam Torrance 73, 69, 68, 70 – 280. Faldo 77, 67, 73, 74 – 291. Jt 26th.

Lawrence Batley International, Bingley St. Ives, Bradford. Faldo 71, 69, 64, 62 – 266. 1st.

Carrolls Irish Open, Royal Dublin. Winner: Seve Ballesteros 67, 67, 70, 67 – 271. Faldo 69, 68, 68, 71 – 276. Jt 3rd.

Benson & Hedges International Open, Fulford GC, York. Winner: John Bland 68, 70, 67, 68 – 273. Faldo 74, 70, 69, 68 – 281. Jt 15th.

Panasonic European Open, Sunningdale, Berkshire. Winner: Isao Aoki 65, 70, 70, 69 – 274. Faldo 68, 69, 68, 71 – 276. Jt 2nd.

Ebel Swiss Open European Masters, Crans-sur-Sierre, Switzerland. Faldo 70, 64, 68, 66 – 268. Tied with Sandy Lyle 64, 63, 70, 71. Faldo defeated Lyle on second extra hole of play-off.

St Mellion Timeshare Tournament Players' Championship, St Mellion G and CC, Plymouth. Winner: Bernhard Langer 69, 68, 66, 66 – 269. Faldo 68, 69, 71, 67 – 275. Jt 6th.

Bob Hope British Classic, Moor Park GC, Rickmansworth. Winner: Jose-Maria Canizares 70, 65, 68, 66 – 269. Faldo 73, 71, 71, 67 – 282. Jt 31st.

Lancome Trophy, St Nom-la-Breteche, Paris. Winner: Seve Ballesteros 71, 65, 64, 69 – 269. Faldo 70, 72, 72, 68 – 282. Jt 15th.

Suntory World Matchplay Championship, The Wentworth Club, Virginia Water. Faldo def. Graham Marsh 2 & 1; Hale Irwin 4 & 3; Bob Charles 6 & 5. Final: Greg Norman def. Faldo 3 & 2.

Bell's Ryder Cup, PGA National GC, Palm Beach, Fla. USA 14½, Europe 13½.First day: Faldo and B. Langer def. L. Wadkins and C. Stadler 4 & 2 (foursomes); Faldo and Langer lost to T. Watson and J. Haas 2 & 1 (fourballs). Second day: Faldo, Langer def. B. Crenshaw, C. Peete 4 & 2 (fourballs); Faldo, Langer def. T. Kite, R. Floyd 3 & 2 (foursomes). Third day: Faldo def. Haas 2 & 1. Faldo won four points out of five.

Order of Merit: 1st   Prize money: £140,751.

1984

Car Care Plan International, Moortown, Leeds. Faldo 69, 70, 66, 71 – 276. 1st.

Peugeot French Open, St Cloud, Paris. Winner: Bernhard Langer 68, 71, 67, 64 – 270. Faldo 71, 68, 66, 68 – 273. 3rd.

Whyte & Mackay PGA, The Wentworth Club, Virginia Water. Winner: H. Clark 64, 69, 71 – 204 (rain stopped play). Faldo 67, 72, 73 – 212. Jt 6th.

Carrolls Irish Open, Royal Dublin. Winner: Bernhard Langer 68, 66, 67, 66 – 267. Faldo 70, 71, 72, 66 – 279. Jt 17th.

Panasonic European Open, Sunningdale, Berkshire. Winner: Gordon Brand Jnr. 67, 66, 73, 64 – 270. Faldo 65, disqualified.

Hennessy Cognac Cup, Ferndown, Dorset. Winners: England, captained by Faldo, def. Spain 3½–2½. Qualifying rds.: Faldo 66, 70. Matchplay Faldo won two singles, halved one fourball and lost one fourball.

Suntory World Matchplay Championship, The Wentworth Club, Virginia Water. Winner: Seve Ballesteros def. Bernhard Langer 2 & 1. First rd: Faldo def. Craig Stadler 3 & 2. Second rd: Ballesteros def. Faldo 4 & 3.

Lancome Trophy, St. Nom-la-Breteche, Paris. Winner: Sandy Lyle 74, 70, 67, 67 – 278. Faldo 74, 74, 71, 69 – 288. Jt 14th.

Order of Merit: 12th   Prize money: £46,054.

Faldo's results world-wide

1976

Sportsman Lager PGA Championship, Wanderers GC, Johannesburg, S. Africa. Winner: Dale Hayes 68, 66, 66, 66 – 266. Faldo 70, 75, 70, 72 – 287. Jt 20th.

Yellow Pages South African Open, Durban Country Club, Durban. Winner: Gary Player 70, 68, 73, 69 – 280. Faldo 76, 74, 72, 75 – 297. Jt 22nd.

Holiday Inns Invitational, Royal Swazi GC, Mbabane, Swaziland. Winner: Hugh Baiocchi 69, 65, 70, 69 – 273 defeating Dale Hayes on fourth hole of play-off. Faldo 69, 70, 76, 71 – 286. Jt 21st.

Rhodesian Dunlop Masters, Royal Salisbury GC, Rhodesia. Winner: Hugh Baiocchi 67, 72, 66, 69 – 274. Faldo 71, 76, 77, 70 – 294. Jt 22nd.

World Open, Pinehurst Country Club, Pinehurst, North Carolina. Winner: Ray Floyd 69, 67, 67, 71 – 274. Faldo, 74, 72 – 146, missed cut.

1977

Moroccan Grand Prix, Royal Dar-es-Salaam GC, Rabat. Winner: Lee Trevino 69, 71, 70, 73 – 283. Faldo 71, 74, 78, 78 – 301. Jt 10th.

World Cup and International Trophy Championship, Wack Wack Golf and Country Club, Manila. Winners: Spain 591. England (Faldo 73, 76, 82, 81 – 312, Peter Dawson 79, 77, 73, 80 – 309) 621. Jt 20th. Individual competition: Faldo jt 44th.

1978

Mayne Nickless PGA Championship of Australia, Royal Melbourne GC, Melbourne. Winner: Hale Irwin 64, 75, 70, 69 – 278. Faldo 71, 75, 77, 76 – 299. Jt 29th.

Wills-Bulletin Australian Open Championship, The Australian GC, Kensington, New South Wales. Winner: Jack Nicklaus 73, 66, 74, 71 – 284. Faldo 80, 73, 77, 77 – 307. Jt 48th.

1979

Kenyan Open, Muthaiga GC, Nairobi. Winner: Maurice Bembridge 67, 65, 69, 70 – 271 defeated Bernard Gallacher on first hole of sudden death play-off. Faldo 68, 73, 68, 70 – 279. Jt 11th.

ICL International, Kensington GC, Johannesburg. Faldo 68, 66, 69, 65 – 268. 1st.

Lexington PGA Championship, Wanderers GC, Johannesburg. Winner: Gary Player 71, 66, 66 – 203. Faldo 70, 73, 72 – 215. Jt 36th.

Kronenbrau '1308', Milnerton GC, Cape Town. Winner: Gary Player 67, 65, 70, 68 – 270. Faldo 65, 70, 70, 76 – 281. 9th.

Yellow Pages-British Airways South African Open, Houghton GC, Johannesburg. Winner: Gary Player 67, 75, 71, 66 – 279. Faldo 72, 73, 71, 75 – 291. Jt 21st.

Sun City Classic, Gary Player CC, Bophuthatswana, South Africa. Winner: Gary Player 70, 71, 67, 70 – 278. Faldo 73, 73, 80, 73 – 299. Jt 29th.

1980

Kenyan Open, Muthaiga Golf Club, Nairobi. Winner: Brian Waites 65, 67, 73, 66 – 271. Faldo 65, 73, 70, 69 – 277. Jt 8th.

Lexington PGA, Wanderers GC, Johannesburg. Winner: Hugh Baiocchi 65, 68, 68, 67 – 268. Faldo 70, 72, 71, 67 – 280. Jt 15th.

ICL International, Kensington GC, Johannesburg. Winner: Harold Henning 73, 67, 69, 72 – 281. Faldo 73, 71, 73, 67 – 284. Jt 5th.

South African Open, Durban Country Club. Winner: Bobby Cole 73, 63, 70, 73 – 279. Faldo 74, 73, 75, 76 – 298. Jt 31st.

Philippine Open, Puerta Azul Beach and Country Club, Ternate. Winner: Lu Hsi Chuen 76, 70, 70, 71 – 287. Faldo failed to qualify.

Cathay Pacific Hong Kong Open, Royal Hong Kong Golf Club, Fanling, Hong Kong. Winner: Kuo Chi Hsiung 72, 67, 68, 67 – 274. Faldo 71, 73, 73, 75 – 292. Jt 36th.

Bridgestone Tournament, Sodegaura CC, Chiba. Winner: Bob Gilder 71, 70, 72, 70 – 283. Faldo 71, 72, 71, 73 – 287. Jt 5th.

1981

Bridgestone, Sodegaura CC, Chiba. Winner: Hale Irwin 70, 65, 72, 68 – 275. Faldo 67, 73, 73, 72 – 285. Jt 4th.

Japan Open, Nihon Line GC, Gifu Prefecture. Winner: Yutaka Hagawa 74, 69, 69, 68 – 280. Faldo 72, 76, 65, 75 – 288. Jt 15th.

1983

Kapalua International, Kapalua Bay GC, Hawaii. Winner: Greg Norman 67, 69, 65, 67 – 268. Faldo 69, 71, 74, 72 – 286. Jt 23rd.

Million Dollar Challenge, Sun City, Bophuthatswana, South Africa. Winner: Seve Ballesteros 69, 67, 70, 68 – 274. Faldo 70, 67, 73, 69 – 279. Jt 2nd.

1984

Australian Masters, Huntingdale, Melbourne. Winner: G. Norman (Australia) 74, 71, 70, 70 – 285. Faldo 73, 74, 71, 74 – 292. 4th.

Bridgestone Tournament, Chiba Prefecture, Japan. Winner: Masahiro Kuramoto (Japan) 67, 74, 67, 71 – 279. Faldo 69, 71, 71, 70 – 281. 8th.

Nissan Cup World Championship, Kurimoto. Winner: Lanny Wadkins (US) 69, 64, 70, 63 – 266. Faldo 70, 70, 69, 69 – 278. 14th.

Kapalua International, Maui, Hawaii. Winner: Sandy Lyle (Scotland) 68, 64, 69, 65 – 266. Faldo 71, 68, 71, 67 – 277. Jt 4th.

Million Dollar Challenge, Sun City, Bophuthatswana, South Africa. Winner: Seve Ballesteros (Spain) 69, 71, 65, 74 – 279. Faldo 70, 72, 71, 72 – 285. 2nd.

South African Airways Masters, Milnerton, Cape Town. Winner: Tony Johnstone (S. Africa) 68, 66, 70, 73 – 277. Faldo 72, 67, 70, 75 – 284. Jt 9th.

Faldo's results in US

1979
Greater Greensboro Open 75, 74, 74, 72 – 295. Jt 44th.
Masters 73, 71, 79, 73 – 296. 40th.

1981
Crosby Natnl. Pro-Am 74, 72, 71 – 217. Jt 37th.
Wickes-Andy Williams-San Diego Open 71, 70, 71, 73 – 285. Jt 32nd.
Hawaiian Open 70, 62, 72, 77 – 281. Jt 40th.
Campbell Los Angeles Open 69, 70, 67, 70 – 276. Jt 9th.
Bay Hill Classic 72, 81, missed cut.
Greater Greensboro Open 72, 73, 68, 69 – 282. 3rd.
Magnolia Classic 70, 66, 73, 68 – 277. Jt 25th.
Tallahassee Open 73, 71, missed cut.
USF & G New Orleans Open 71, 70, 73, 68 – 282. Jt 34th.
Michelob Houston Open 69, 69, 82 – 220 (rain stopped play). Jt 79th.
World Series 74, 73, 72, 72 – 291. 21st.

1982
Phoenix Open 73, 70, 74, 74 – 291. 73rd.
Wickes-Andy Williams-San Diego Open 69, 69, 69, 73 – 280. Jt 24th.
Crosby Natnl. Pro-Am 75, 72, 73 – 220 (rain stopped play). Jt 61st.
Hawaiian Open 73, 67, 73, 68 – 281. Jt 7th.
Campbell Los Angeles Open 75, 68, 74, 75 – 292. Jt 66th.
Doral-Eastern Open 68, 72, 73, 71 – 284. Jt 11th.
Bay Hill Classic 72, 67, 73, 71 – 283. 17th.
Tournament Players' Championship 75, 70, 75, 74 – 294. Jt 35th.
Sea Pines Heritage Classic 69, 73, 74, 72 – 288. Jt 21st.
Greater Greensboro Open 75, 71, 74, 74 – 294. Jt 18th.
Magnolia Classic 68, 71, 70, 68 – 277. Jt 15th.
Tallahassee Open 73, 73, missed cut.
USF & G Classic 75, 72, missed cut.
Canadian Open 68, 70, 73, 70 – 281. Jt 5th.
PGA Championship 67, 70, 73, 72 – 282. Jt 14th.

1983
Phoenix Open 77, 65, missed cut.
Crosby Natnl. Pro-Am 71, 75, 73, missed cut.
Hawaiian Open 69, 70, 72, 74 – 285. Jt 60th.
Isuzu-Andy Williams-San Diego Open 70, 75, missed cut.

Doral-Eastern Open 70, 70, 73, 75 – 288. Jt 42nd.
USF & G Classic 72, 70, 74, 68 – 284. Jt 22nd.
Tournament Players' Championship 74, 74, 72, 75 – 295. Jt 35th.
Greater Greensboro Open 71, 71, 71, 70 – 283. 6th.
The Masters 70, 70, 76, 76 – 292. Jt 20th.
Sea Pines Heritage Classic 73, 74, missed cut.
Byron Nelson Golf Classic 71, 69, 72, 69 – 281. Jt 21st.
PGA Championship 74, 77, missed cut.
Walt Disney World Golf Classic 72, 65, 68, 66 – 271. Jt 2nd.

1984

Bob Hope Classic 72, 71, 70, 69, 70 – 352. Jt 30th.
Phoenix Open 72, 67, 70, 68 – 277. Jt 27th.
Isuzu-Andy Williams-San Diego Open 70, 71, 72, 67 – 280. Jt 35th.
Crosby Natnl. Pro-Am 70, 72, 71, 68 – 281. 5th.
Hawaiian Open 74, 72, missed cut.
Honda Classic 79, 68, 67, 72 – 286. Jt 12th.
Doral-Eastern Open 70, 75, missed cut.
Bay Hill Classic 72, 68, 68, 72 – 280. Jt 9th.
Tournament Players' Championship 73, 73, 74, 69 – 289. Jt 20th.
Greater Greensboro Open 71, 70, 73, 72 – 286. Jt 8th.
The Masters 70, 69, 70, 76 – 285. Jt 15th.
Sea Pines Heritage Classic 66, 67, 68, 69 – 270. 1st.
Mony Tournament of Champions 73, 72, 71, 74 – 290. Jt 17th.
Manufacturers Hanover Westchester Classic 74, 76, missed cut.
US Open 71, 76, 77, 72 – 296. Jt 55th.
Georgia-Pacific Atlanta Classic 77, 72, missed cut.
Canadian Open 76, 75, missed cut.
PGA Championship 69, 73, 74, 70 – 286. Jt 20th.
World Series 73, 71, 71, 72 – 287. Jt 26th.

Index